FTCE Middle Grades Social Science 5-9

Teacher Certification Exam

By: Sharon Wynne, M.S.
Southern Connecticut State University

"And, while there's no reason yet to panic, I think it's only prudent that we make preparations to panic."

XAMonline, INC.
Boston

XAMonline, Inc.
25 First Street, Suite 106
Cambridge, MA 02141
Toll Free 1-800-509-4128
Email: info@xamonline.com
Web www.xamonline.com
Fax: 1-617-583-5552

Library of Congress Cataloging-in-Publication Data
Wynne, Sharon A.
     Middle Grades Social Science 5-9: Teacher Certification / Sharon A. Wynne. -3rd ed.
     ISBN 978-1-60787-010-4
     1. Middle Grades Social Science 5-9. 2. Study Guides. 3. FTCE 4. Teachers' Certification & Licensure.   5. Careers

Managine Editor   Dr. Harte Weiner, Ph. D.
Copy Editor   James Stark, M.A.
Assistant Editor   Kerrie Forbes, B.A.

Disclaimer:
The opinions expressed in this publication are the sole works of XAMonline and were created independently from the National Education Association, Educational Testing Service, or any State Department of Education, National Evaluation Systems or other testing affiliates. Between the time of publication and printing, state specific standards as well as testing formats and website information may change that is not included in part or in whole within this product. Sample test questions are developed by XAMonline and reflect similar content as on real tests; however, they are not former tests. XAMonline assembles content that aligns with state standards but makes no claims nor guarantees teacher candidates a passing score. Numerical scores are determined by testing companies such as NES or ETS and then are compared with individual state standards. A passing score varies from state to state.

Printed in the United States of America   œ-1
FTCE: Middle Grades Social Science 5-9
ISBN: 978-1-60787-010-4

About the Subject Assessments

FTCE™: Subject Assessment in the Middle Grades Social Science 5-9 examination

Purpose: The assessments are designed to test the knowledge and competencies of prospective secondary level teachers. The question bank from which the assessment is drawn is undergoing constant revision. As a result, your test may include questions that will not count towards your score.

Test Version: There are two versions of subject assessments for social science tests in Florida. Although both versions of the test emphasize conceptual comprehension, synthesis, and analysis of the principles of the social sciences, the major difference between versions lays in the *degree* to which the examinee's knowledge is tested.

Version 1: Social Science 6-12 This version requires a greater depth of comprehension in US History, world history, economics, geography, political science, anthropology and psychology. The social science 6-12 guide is based on a typical knowledge level of persons who have completed a _bachelor's degree program_ in social science.

Version 2: Middle Grades Social Science 5-9 This version test the examinee's knowledge level in less detail than the first version of the subject assessments. The degree of knowledge required is typically based on completion of _introductory-level course work_ in the same areas mentioned above. Although US History remains the focus of both tests there are fewer questions on that topic in Social Science 5-9.

Taking the Correct Version of the Subject Assessment: While some states other than Florida offer just one test called a social science secondary test, Florida breaks out those topics into two tests. The 5-9 is basically what you would take to become a middle school teacher and 6-12 if you plan on teaching at the high school level. However, as Florida's licensure requirements change, it's highly recommended that you consult your educational institution's teaching preparation counselor or your state board of education's teacher licensure division, to verify which version of the assessment you should take. Not mentioned is a History test. If you plan on applying for a position in another state as well as Florida consider a History option. XAMonline.com website can inform you what you need to do to become certified in any particular state.

Time Allowance, Format, and Length: The time allowance and format for both versions are identical; you will have 2 hours to complete the test and the questions are presented in a 125 question multiple-choice format. Florida does not test using construct essays or other essay formats.

Content Areas: Both versions of the subject assessments share a degree of commonality in that the test content categories are divided into (6) broad areas that roughly overlap between test versions. However, version (1) has a narrower focus on specific disciplines than does version (2).

Test Taxonomy: Both versions of the subject assessments are constructed on the comprehension, synthesis and analysis levels of Bloom's Taxonomy. In many questions, the candidate must apply knowledge of more than one discipline in order to correctly answer the questions.

Additional Information about the FTCE Assessments: The FTCE™ series subject assessments are developed by the *Florida Department of Education* of Tallahassee, FL. They provide additional information on the FTCE series assessments, including registration, preparation and testing procedures, study materials such as topical guides that are about 30 pages of information including approximately 25 additional sample questions.

TABLE OF CONTENTS

Great Study and Testing Tips!

What to study in order to prepare for the subject assessments is the focus of this study guide but equally important is *how* you study.

You can increase your chances of truly mastering the information by taking some simple, but effective steps.

Study Tips:

1. Some foods aid the learning process. Foods such as milk, nuts, seeds, rice, and oats help your study efforts by releasing natural memory enhancers called CCKs (*cholecystokinin*) composed of *tryptophan*, *choline*, and *phenylalanine*. All of these chemicals enhance the neurotransmitters associated with memory. Before studying, try a light, protein-rich meal of eggs, turkey, and fish. All of these foods release the memory enhancing chemicals. The better the connections, the more you comprehend.

Likewise, before you take a test, stick to a light snack of energy boosting and relaxing foods. A glass of milk, a piece of fruit, or some peanuts all release various memory-boosting chemicals and help you to relax and focus on the subject at hand.

2. Learn to take great notes. A by-product of our modern culture is that we have grown accustomed to getting our information in short doses (i.e. TV news sound bites or USA Today style newspaper articles.)

Consequently, we've subconsciously trained ourselves to assimilate information better in neat little packages. If your notes are scrawled all over the paper, it fragments the flow of the information. Strive for clarity. Newspapers use a standard format to achieve clarity. Your notes can be much clearer through use of proper formatting. A very effective format is called the *"Cornell Method."*

> Take a sheet of loose-leaf lined notebook paper and draw a line all the way down the paper about 1-2" from the left-hand edge.
>
> Draw another line across the width of the paper about 1-2" up from the bottom. Repeat this process on the reverse side of the page.

Look at the highly effective result. You have ample room for notes, a left hand margin for special emphasis items or inserting supplementary data from the textbook, a large area at the bottom for a brief summary, and a little rectangular space for just about anything you want.

3. <u>Get the concept then the details.</u> Too often we focus on the details and don't gather an understanding of the concept. However, if you simply memorize only dates, places, or names, you may well miss the whole point of the subject.

A key way to understand things is to put them in your own words. If you are working from a textbook, automatically summarize each paragraph in your mind. If you are outlining text, don't simply copy the author's words.

Rephrase them in your own words. You remember your own thoughts and words much better than someone else's, and subconsciously tend to associate the important details to the core concepts.

4. <u>Ask Why?</u> Pull apart written material paragraph by paragraph and don't forget the captions under the illustrations.

Example: If the heading is "Stream Erosion", flip it around to read "Why do streams erode?" Then answer the questions.

If you train your mind to think in a series of questions and answers, not only will you learn more, but it also helps to lessen the test anxiety because you are used to answering questions.

5. <u>Read for reinforcement and future needs.</u> Even if you only have 10 minutes, put your notes or a book in your hand. Your mind is similar to a computer; you have to input data in order to have it processed. *By reading, you are creating the neural connections for future retrieval.* The more times you read something, the more you reinforce the learning of ideas.

Even if you don't fully understand something on the first pass, *your mind stores much of the material for later recall.*

6. <u>Relax to learn so go into exile.</u> Our bodies respond to an inner clock called biorhythms. Burning the midnight oil works well for some people, but not everyone.

If possible, set aside a particular place to study that is free of distractions. Shut off the television, cell phone, pager and exile your friends and family during your study period.

If you really are bothered by silence, try background music. Light classical music at a low volume has been shown to aid in concentration over other types. Music that evokes pleasant emotions without lyrics are highly suggested. Try just about anything by Mozart. It relaxes you.

7. <u>Use arrows not highlighters.</u> At best, it's difficult to read a page full of yellow, pink, blue, and green streaks.

Try staring at a neon sign for a while and you'll soon see my point, the horde of colors obscure the message.
A quick note, a brief dash of color, an underline, and an arrow pointing to a particular passage is much clearer than a horde of highlighted words.

8. Budget your study time. Although you shouldn't ignore any of the material, *allocate your available study time in the same ratio that topics may appear on the test.*

Testing Tips:

1. Get smart, play dumb. Don't read anything into the question. Don't make an assumption that the test writer is looking for something else than what is asked. Stick to the question as written and don't read extra things into it.

2. Read the question and all the choices *twice* before answering the question. You may miss something by not carefully reading, and then re-reading both the question and the answers.

If you really don't have a clue as to the right answer, leave it blank on the first time through. Go on to the other questions, as they may provide a clue as to how to answer the skipped questions.

If later on, you still can't answer the skipped ones . . . *Guess.*
The only penalty for guessing is that you *might* get it wrong. Only one thing is certain; if you don't put anything down, you will get it wrong!

3. Turn the question into a statement. Look at the way the questions are worded. The syntax of the question usually provides a clue. Does it seem more familiar as a statement rather than as a question? Does it sound strange?

By turning a question into a statement, you may be able to spot if an answer sounds right, and it may also trigger memories of material you have read.

4. Look for hidden clues. It's actually very difficult to compose multiple-foil (choice) questions without giving away part of the answer in the options presented.

In most multiple-choice questions you can often readily eliminate one or two of the potential answers. This leaves you with only two real possibilities and automatically your odds go to Fifty-Fifty for very little work.

5. Trust your instincts. For every fact that you have read, you subconsciously retain something of that knowledge. On questions that you aren't really certain about, go with your basic instincts. **Your first impression on how to answer a question is usually correct.**

6. Mark your answers directly on the test booklet. Don't bother trying to fill in the optical scan sheet on the first pass through the test.

Just be very careful not to miss-mark your answers when you eventually transcribe them to the scan sheet.

7. Watch the clock! You have a set amount of time to answer the questions. Don't get bogged down trying to answer a single question at the expense of 10 questions you can more readily answer.

COMPETENCY 1.0   KNOWLEDGE OF HISTORY

Skill 1.1   Identify major historical events and how they are related by cause and effect.

The **Renaissance** ushered in a time of curiosity, learning, and incredible energy sparking the desire for trade to procure these new, exotic products and to find better, faster, cheaper trade routes to get to them. The work of geographers, astronomers and mapmakers made important contributions and many studied and applied the work of such men as Hipparchus of Greece, Ptolemy of Egypt, Tycho Brahe of Denmark, and Fra Mauro of Italy.

The **Scientific Revolution** was characterized by a shift in scientific approach and ideas. Near the end of the 16th century, Galileo Galilei introduced a radical approach to the study of motion. He moved from attempts to explain why objects move the way they do and began to use experiments to describe precisely how they move. He also used experimentation to describe how forces affect non-moving objects. Other scientists continued in the same approach. Outstanding scientists of the period included Johannes Kepler, Evangelista Torricelli, Blaise Pascal, Isaac Newton and Leibniz. This was the period when experiments dominated scientific study. This method was particularly applied to the study of physics.

The **Agricultural Revolution** occurred first in England. It was marked by experimentation that resulted in increased production of crops from the land and a new and more technical approach to the management of agriculture. The revolution in agricultural management and production was hugely enhanced by the Industrial Revolution and the invention of the steam engine. The introduction of steam-powered tractors greatly increased crop production and significantly decreased labor costs. Developments in agriculture were also enhanced by the Scientific Revolution and the learning from experimentation that led to philosophies of crop rotation and soil enrichment. Improved systems of irrigation and harvesting also contributed to the growth of agricultural production.

The **Industrial Revolution**, which began in Great Britain and spread elsewhere, was the development of power-driven machinery (fueled by coal and steam) leading to the accelerated growth of industry with large factories replacing homes and small workshops as work centers. The lives of people changed drastically and a largely agricultural society changed to an industrial one. In Western Europe, the period of empire and colonialism began. The industrialized nations seized and claimed parts of Africa and Asia in an effort to control and provide the raw materials needed to feed the industries and machines in the "mother country". Later developments included power-based electricity and internal combustion, replacing coal and steam.

Skill 1.2 **Analyze examples of primary source documents for historical perspective.**

Primary sources include the following kinds of materials:

Documents that reflect the immediate, everyday concerns of people: memoranda, bills, deeds, charters, newspaper reports, pamphlets, graffiti, popular writings, journals or diaries, records of decision-making bodies, letters, receipts, snapshots, etc.

Theoretical writings which reflect care and consideration in composition and an attempt to convince or persuade. The topic will generally be deeper and more pervasive values than is the case with "immediate" documents. These may include newspaper or magazine editorials, sermons, political speeches, philosophical writings, etc.

Narrative accounts of events, ideas, trends, etc. written with intention by someone contemporary with the events described.

Statistical data, although statistics may be misleading.

Literature and nonverbal materials, novels, stories, poetry and essays from the period, as well as coins, archaeological artifacts, and art produced during the period. Guidelines for the use of primary resources:

1. Be certain that you understand how language was used at the time of writing and that you understand the context in which it was produced.
2. Do not read history blindly; be certain that you understand both explicit and implicit referenced in the material.
3. Read the entire text you are reviewing; do not simply extract a few sentences to read.
4. Although anthologies of materials may help you identify primary source materials, the full original text should be consulted.

Secondary sources include the following kinds of materials:

- Books written on the basis of primary materials about the period of time
- Books written on the basis of primary materials about persons who played a major role in the events under consideration
- Books and articles written on the basis of primary materials about the culture, the social norms, the language, and the values of the period
- Quotations from primary sources
- Statistical data on the period
- The conclusions and inferences of other historians
- Multiple interpretations of the ethos of the time

Guidelines for the use of secondary sources:

- Do not rely upon only a single secondary source.
- Check facts and interpretations against primary sources whenever possible.
- Do not accept the conclusions of other historians uncritically.
- Place greatest reliance on secondary sources created by the best and most respected scholars.
- Do not use the inferences of other scholars as if they were facts.
- Ensure that you recognize any bias the writer brings to his/her interpretation of history.
- Understand the primary point of the book as a basis for evaluating the value of the material presented in it to your questions.

Skill 1.3   **Identify cultural, political, social, economic, and technological contributions made by civilizations in Africa, the Americas, Asia (including the Middle East), Europe, and Oceania.**

For example:

Renaissance

Art - The more important artists were **Giotto** and his development of perspective in paintings; **Leonardo Da Vinci** was not only an artist but also a scientist and inventor; **Michelangelo** was a sculptor, painter, and architect; and others include **Raphael**, **Donatello**, **Titian**, and **Tintoretto**

Political philosophy - the writings of **Machiavelli**

Literature - the writings of **Petrarch** and **Boccaccio**

Science - **Galileo**

Medicine - The work of Brussels-born **Andrea Vesalius** earned him the title of "father of anatomy" and had a profound influence on the Spaniard **Michael Servetus** and the Englishman **William Harvey**

In Germany, Gutenberg's invention of the **printing press** with movable type facilitated the rapid spread of Renaissance ideas, writings and innovations, thus ensuring the enlightenment of most of Western Europe. Contributions were also made by Durer and Holbein in art and by Paracelsus in science and medicine.

*The effects of the Renaissance in the Low Countries can be seen in the literature and philosophy of **Erasmus** and the art of **van Eyck** and **Breughel the Elder**. **Rabelais** and **de Montaigne** in France also contributed to literature and philosophy. In Spain, the art of **El Greco** and **de Morales** flourished as did the writings of **Cervantes** and **De Vega**. In England, **Sir Thomas More** and **Sir Francis Bacon** wrote and taught philosophy and were inspired by **Vesalius**. **William Harvey** made important contributions in medicine. The greatest talent was found in literature and drama and given to mankind by **Chaucer, Spenser, Marlowe, Jonson**, and the incomparable **Shakespeare**.*

The Renaissance ushered in a time of curiosity, learning, and incredible energy sparking the desire for trade to procure these new, exotic products and to find better, faster, cheaper trade routes to get to them. The work of geographers, astronomers and mapmakers made important contributions and many studied and applied the work of such men as Hipparchus of Greece, Ptolemy of Egypt, Tycho Brahe of Denmark, and Fra Mauro of Italy.

Skill 1.4 Relate major historical events and movements to physical and human geographic factors.

Genocide is defined by the **Convention on the Prevention and Punishment of the Crime of Genocide** (CPPCG):

> **Article II:** In the present Convention, genocide means any of the following acts committed with intent to destroy, in whole or in part, a national, ethnical, racial or religious group, as such:
>
> (a) Killing members of the group;
> (b) Causing serious bodily or mental harm to members of the group;
> (c) Deliberately inflicting on the group conditions of life calculated to bring about its physical destruction in whole or in part;
> (d) Imposing measures intended to prevent births within the group;
> (e) Forcibly transferring children of the group to another group.

Notable instances of genocide have occurred throughout history and throughout the world.

In the United States, efforts to claim and expand the territory of the new nation and its perceived rights to settle the nation led to the attempted extermination of the Native American peoples. To be sure, many died from diseases introduced by European settlers against which the Native Americans had no acquired or natural resistance. The Native Americians were, however, systematically pushed west—out of the way of progress and national development. They were relocated to undesirable lands where many starved. The most systematic efforts, however, occurred in the Indian Wars when entire villages and tribes were wantonly slaughtered. The massacre at **Wounded Knee** (1890) is a memorable example of this policy.

During the reign of the Ottoman Empire, the government of the Young Turks, 1915-1917 forced the mass evacuation of over one million Armenians. Many died or were executed in the process. This is referred to as the **Armenian Genocide**, and indeed the term was coined to describe the event. The Armenians were Christians in a Muslim empire. When the Russians defeated the Ottoman Empire in 1915, the Young Turks placed the blame on the Armenians.

The **Holocaust** was an effort at ethnic cleansing of Germany and Europe by Adolf Hitler and the Nazi government. Millions of Jews and other "undesirables" were gathered from throughout Europe as the German army advanced and sent to concentration camps where they were either used for medical experimentation, slave labor, or exterminated. Most of the world was slow to believe that this kind of genocide could be occurring, and therefore slow to respond. Hundreds of thousands of Jews were murdered in the gas chambers of the camps.

The genocides in **Bosnia-Herzegovina** and **Rwanda** were two sides of the same story, one of the oldest in the world, that of one ethnic group trying to eliminate another solely because of its ethnicity. The disparity between the number of people killed in these two modern **genocides** in no way reflects any difference in ferocity with which these people were murdered.

The Bosnian Genocide, as it is usually called, took place during the Bosnian War, which lasted from 1992 to 1995. It was part of a larger conflict that stemmed from the breakup of Yugoslavia, which was itself a confederation of ethnic societies held together by not much more than an iron fist for most of its life. Bosnia-Herzegovina and Serbia were once and again their own countries, and their ethnic conflict stretched back for ages. With modern weapons, however, the "ethnic cleansing" that the Serbs practiced on their Bosnian neighbors reached new heights of efficiency.

The worst group of mass murders on record is that at **Srebenica**, in 1992, when, international observers estimate, Serbs murdered more than 8,000 Bosnians. The people of Bosnia-Herzegovina say that Srebenica was just one of many such instances of genocide. Some reports have deaths numbering in the hundreds of thousands, with millions forced to flee their homes.

Serbia also maintained detainment camps during this war that practiced cruel and unusual punishment of prisoners. Photos of some of these detainees made the rounds in international circles during the war, strengthening Bosnia's case against Serb oppression.

As more and more details of the Serb atrocities leaked out, the international outcry over such events grew stronger and stronger. United Nations forces were eventually sent to restore order.

In the end, Serbia was made to stop its "cleansing." The reason given for such atrocities was multi-faceted, but they were all facets of the same basic cause: one ethnic group determined to stamp out another.

The same was true in **Rwanda**, where Hutus systematically murdered close to a million Tutsis. This staggering number included fellow Hutus who were sympathetic to the Tutsi cause. Most shocking of all, this genocide took place in about 100 days, in the spring and summer of 1994. Perhaps world opinion was too much divided over how to respond to the Serbian problem; perhaps no one cared "because it's only Africa." Whatever the reason, it took other nations of the world a relatively long time to respond to such savagery.

The Rwandan Genocide was more a matter of geography and economics, as Hutus coveted land owned and worked by Tutsis. Rwanda then, as now, was also a densely populated country, but only in certain areas. The ownership of much of those areas was in dispute, a dispute that spanned centuries of cohabitation and colonization.

International opinion eventually focused on Rwanda, however, and the killings were brought to a halt—not before the aforementioned million people died, however. Again, the impetus for the killings was competing ethnicities.

Another tremendously oppressive ethnic conflict is taking place in the **Darfur** region of **Sudan**. An organized campaign of Janjaweed militia has been persecuting members of ethnic groups Fur, Zaghawa, and Massalit, among others. Some estimates put the death toll higher than two million and the number of displaced people higher than four million. The killing goes on in Darfur, with little repercussion from the outside world.

The African genocides fly in the face of Pan-Africanism, the belief that all Africans are one and that they should expand their solidarity under that maxim. The philosophy is a rather old one that has seen new life in recent decades, most notably in Ethiopia and South Africa. Many social scientists argue that if this doctrine were followed, such genocides as those in Rwanda and Sudan would not take place. These social scientists would argue that Africans should respect the lives, intentions, and ethnicities of their fellow Africans.

The same sort of cultural nationalism can be found in the doctrine of Pan-Arabism, which is the call for Arab peoples to unite as Arabs and put political, ethnic, and religious differences behind them in favor of a unity based on joint heritage and shared tradition. This doctrine was in force much more prominently in the early days of Islam and saw its zenith during the Crusades. Even then, though, divides in the Muslim world were deep for many Arabs. Those rifts have widened as the centuries have gone by, and many social scientists question whether Pan-Arabism would gain many adherents in the modern, fragmented world. Indeed, many would argue that Pan-Africanism is more likely to succeed than Pan-Arabism, simply because of geography.

At the turn of the twenty-first century, the world witnessed unprecedented strides in communications, a major expansion of international trade, and significant international diplomatic and military activity.

Globalism is defined as the principle of the interdependence of all the world's nations and their peoples. Within this global community, every nation, in some way to a certain degree, is dependent on other nations. Since no one nation has all of the resources needed for production, trade with other nations is required to obtain what is needed for production, to sell what is produced or to buy finished products, and to earn money to maintain and strengthen the nation's economic system.

Developing nations receive technical assistance and financial aid from developed nations. Many international organizations have been created to promote and encourage cooperation and economic progress among member nations. Through the elimination of barriers to trade such as tariffs, trade is stimulated, resulting in increased productivity, economic progress, cooperation, and understanding on diplomatic levels.

Nations not part of an international trade organization not only must make economic decisions of what to produce, how and for whom, but must also deal with the problem of tariffs and quotas on imports. Regardless of international trade memberships, economic growth and development are vital and affect all trading nations. Businesses, labor, and governments share common interests and goals in a nation's economic status. International systems of banking and finance have been devised to assist governments and businesses in setting the policy and guidelines for the exchange of currencies.

The global economy had its origins in the early twentieth century, with the advent of the airplane, which made travel and trade easier and less time-consuming than ever. With the recent advent of the Internet, the world might be better termed a global neighborhood.

The speed of airplanes results in not only shorter tourist trips but also shorter trade trips, meaning that goods (especially perishable foods) can travel farther and wider than ever before. Being able to ship goods quickly and efficiently means that businesses can conduct business overseas much more efficiently than they ever could.

Trucks, trains, and ships carry cargo all over the world. Trains travel faster than ever, as do ships. Roads are more prevalent and usually in better repair than they have ever been, making truck and even car travel not the dead-end option that it once was.

With all of this capability has come increasing demand. People traditionally had exchanged goods using their own means of transportation or from traders who lived nearby. As technology improved, trade routes expanded and imports from overseas grew. This demand feeds the economic imperative of creating more supply—and vice versa. As more people discover goods from overseas, the demand for those foreign goods increases. Because people can get goods from overseas with relative ease, they continue to get them and demand more. Suppliers are only too happy to supply the goods.

An incredible increase in demand for something is not always a good thing, however, especially if what is being demanded is in limited supply. The precious rainforests are disappearing at an alarming rate, especially in South America and Indonesia. Not only do rainforests provide products, but they are an essential part of the global weather system.

Nonrenewable resources such as coal and oil are in worldwide demand these days, and the supplies won't last forever. Making it easier to ship goods all over the world has made demand grow at an unbelievable rate, raising concerns about supply. Because resources like this have a limited supply (even though the day when that limit is reached seems far away still), they are in danger of becoming extinct without being replaced.

Globalization has also brought about welcome and unwelcome developments in the field of epidemiology. Vaccines and other cures for diseases can be shipped relatively quickly all around the world. For example, this has made it possible for HIV vaccines to reach the remotest areas of the world, for example. Unfortunately, the preponderance of global travel has also meant that the threat of spreading a disease to the world by an infected person traveling on an international flight is quite real.

Technology contributed to globalization with the development of the **Internet**. Instant communication between people thousands of miles apart is possible just by plugging in a computer and connecting to the Internet. The Internet is an extension of the telephone and cell phone revolutions; all three are developments in communications that have brought faraway places closer together. All three allow people to communicate no matter the distance. This communication can facilitate friendly chatter, remote business meetings, and distant trade opportunities. Cell phones and the Internet are often required to do business nowadays. Computer programs enable the tracking of goods and receipts quickly and efficiently.

Globalization has also brought financial and cultural exchange on a worldwide scale. Many businesses have investments in countries around the world. Financial transactions are conducted using a variety of currencies. The cultures of the countries of the world are increasingly viewed by people throughout the world via multimedia developments. Not only goods but also belief systems, customs, and practices are being exchanged.

With this exchange of money, goods, and culture has come an increase in immigration. Many people who live in less-developed nations see what is available in other places and want to move there, in order to fully take advantage of all that those more-developed nations have to offer. This can create an increase in immigration. Depending on the numbers of people who want to immigrate and the resources available, this could become a problem. The technological advances in transportation and communications have made such immigration easier than ever.

Skill 1.5   Identify significant historical leaders and events and their influence on world civilizations.

The Age of Exploration actually had its beginnings centuries before exploration actually took place. The rise and spread of Islam in the seventh century and its subsequent control over the holy city of Jerusalem led to the European so-called Holy Wars, the Crusades, to free Jerusalem and the Holy Land from this control. Even though the Crusades were not a success, those who survived and returned to their homes and countries in Western Europe brought back with them new products such as silks, spices, perfumes, new and different foods—luxuries that were unheard of and that gave new meaning what may have to colorless, drab, dull lives.

New ideas, new inventions, and new methods also went to Western Europe with the returning Crusaders, and from these new influences was the intellectual stimulation which led to the period known as the Renaissance. The revival of interest in classical Greek art, classical Greek architecture, classical Greek literature—and developments in science, astronomy, medicine along with increased trade between Europe and Asia—and the invention of the printing press helped to push the spread of knowledge and stimulated more global exploration.

For many centuries, mapmakers made many maps and charts, which in turn stimulated curiosity and the seeking of more knowledge. At the same time, the Chinese were using the magnetic compass in their ships. Pacific islanders were going from island to island, covering thousands of miles in open canoes navigating by sun and stars. Arab traders were sailing all over the Indian Ocean in their dhows. The trade routes between Europe and Asia were slow, difficult, dangerous, and very expensive. Between sea voyages on the Indian Ocean and Mediterranean Sea and the camel caravans in central Asia and the Arabian Desert, the trade was still controlled by the Italian merchants in Genoa and Venice. It would take months and even years for the exotic luxuries of Asia to reach the markets of Western Europe. A faster, cheaper way had to be found. A way had to be found which would bypass traditional routes and end the control of the Italian merchants.

Prince Henry of Portugal (also called the Navigator) encouraged, supported, and financed the Portuguese seamen who led in the search for an all-water route to Asia. A shipyard was built along with a school that taught navigation. New types of sailing ships were built which would carry the seamen safely through the ocean waters. Experiments were conducted in newer maps, newer navigational methods, and newer instruments. These included the astrolabe and the compass enabling sailors to determine direction as well as latitude and longitude for exact location. Although Prince Henry died in 1460, the Portuguese kept on, sailing and exploring Africa's west coastline. In 1488, Bartholomew Diaz and his men sailed around Africa's southern tip and headed toward Asia. Diaz wanted to push on but turned back because his men were discouraged and weary from the long months at sea, extremely fearful of the unknown, and unwilling to travel any further.

However, the Portuguese were finally successful ten years later in 1498 when Vasco da Gama and his men, continuing the route of Diaz, rounded Africa's Cape of Good Hope, sailing across the Indian Ocean, reaching India's port of Calicut (Calcutta). Although, six years earlier, Columbus had reached the New World and an entire hemisphere, da Gama had proved Asia could be reached from Europe by sea.

Columbus' first trans-Atlantic voyage proved his theory that Asia could be reached by sailing west. It could be done—but only after figuring how to go around or across or through the landmass in between. Long after Spain dispatched explorers and her famed conquistadors to gather the wealth for the Spanish monarchs and their coffers, the British were searching valiantly for the "Northwest Passage," a land-sea route across North America and open sea to the wealth of Asia. It wasn't until after the Lewis and Clark Expedition when Captains Meriwether Lewis and William Clark proved conclusively that there simply was no Northwest Passage..

ROUTES OF THE ARMADA
X Fights in the channel
Wrecks

However, this did not deter exploration and settlement. Spain, France, and England along with some participation by the Dutch led the way with expanding Western European civilization in the New World. These three nations had strong monarchial governments and were struggling for dominance and power in Europe. With the defeat of Spain's mighty Armada in 1588, England became undisputed mistress of the seas. Spain lost its power and influence in Europe and it was left to France and England to carry on the rivalry, leading to eventual British control in Asia as well.

Spain's influence was in Florida, the Gulf Coast from Texas all the way west to California and south to the tip of South America and to some of the islands of the West Indies. French control centered from New Orleans north to what is now northern Canada including the entire Mississippi Valley, the St. Lawrence Valley, the Great Lakes, and the land that was part of the Louisiana Territory. A few West Indies islands were also part of France's empire. England settled the eastern seaboard of North America, including parts of Canada and from Maine to Georgia. Some West Indies islands also came under British control. The Dutch had New Amsterdam for a period of time but later ceded it into British hands.

For each of these three nations—Spain, France, and especially England—the land claims extended partly or all the way across the continent, no matter that others claimed the same land. The wars for dominance and control of power and influence in Europe eventually extended to the Americas, especially North America.

The importance of the Age of Exploration was not just the discovery and colonization of the New World, but better maps and charts and newer and more accurate navigational instruments increased knowledge and great wealth. Furthermore, new and different foods and other items previously unknown in Europe were introduced. A new hemisphere became accessible as a refuge from poverty and persecution—a place to start a new and better life. The proof that Asia could be reached by sea and that the earth was round meant that ships and sailors would not sail off the edge of a flat earth and disappear forever into nothingness.

A nation-state is a political state where territorial and national boundaries coincide. Prior to the development of the nation-state, people banded together based on similar culture and language in what could be called a nation of people. The areas where these nations of people lived might be widespread or narrow, with no political boundaries—or loose boundaries that fluctuated. Eventually, the idea arose that a nation of people could claim a specific defined territory with boundaries within which that nation's laws and customs were sovereign. In addition, this sovereign nation held an individual identity in relation to other similar nations. This pairing of national identity with political identity is what defines a nation-state.

How the nation-state came in to existence is a subject debated among social scientists. However, there are some important historical events that point to its development. The **Peace of Westphalia**, in 1648, refers to the signing of two treaties that ended longtime warring among the peoples of Europe. The treaties spelled out several principles that are now thought of as crucial components of the modern nation-state:

- States had the right of self-determination and were sovereign
- States were equal in regard to one another
- States should not interfere with the internal affairs of other states

These principles are still at the core of international relations. The modern system of sovereign states is still referred to as the "Westphalian System."

Capitalism is closely tied to the principle of the nation-state, and some theories tie the development of the nation-state to the rise of capitalism. As industry replaced agriculture in the economic realm, the nation-state arose to meet the needs of industry, such as the construction of roads and ports and the abolishment of tariffs and trade restrictions within its borders. The concept of national sovereignty over a specific territory had a corollary for the individual: personal property rights. A nation-state with laws protecting private property is essential for the growth of capitalism.

The concept of the nation-state has been the basis of important political movements that have had widespread impact on world history. In the 19th century, Prussia, under the leadership of Otto von Bismarck and Wilhelm I, rallied the various Germanic states of Europe around the notion of a sovereign territory in opposition to the Austria-Hungary Empire. This growing surge of nationalism among the sovereign nation-states of Europe eventually led to the complex series of treaties and agreements that unraveled to produce the First World War. Later in the twentieth century in Germany, Adolf Hitler claimed sovereignty over adjoining territory based on the national character of the nation-state, leading to the Second World War.

The period from the 1700s to the 1800s was characterized in Western countries by opposing political ideas of democracy and nationalism. This resulted in strong nationalistic feelings and people of common cultures asserting their belief in the right to have a part in their government.

The **American Revolution** resulted in the successful efforts of the English colonists in America to win their freedom from Great Britain. After more than one hundred years of mostly self-government, the colonists resented the increased British meddling and control. They declared their freedom, won the Revolutionary War with aid from France, and formed a new independent nation.

The American colonists were striking back against British unwanted taxation and other sorts of "government interference." The French people were starving and, in many cases, destitute. They rebelled against an autocratic regime that cared more for high fashion and "courtly love" than food and health for the people..

- The American Revolution involved a year-long campaign, of bloody battles, skirmishes, and stalemates. The French Revolution was bloody to a degree but mainly an overthrow of society and its outdated traditions.
- The American Revolution resulted in a representative government, which marketed itself as a beacon of democracy for the rest of the world. The French Revolution resulted in a consulship, a generalship, and then an emperor—probably not what the perpetrators of the Revolution had in mind when they first rose against King Louis XVI and Queen Marie-Antoinette.

The major turning point for **Latin America**, already unhappy with Spanish restrictions on trade, agriculture, and the manufacture of goods, was Napoleon's move into Spain and Portugal. Napoleon's imprisonment of King Ferdinand VII made the local agents of the Spanish authorities feel that they were agents of the French. Conservative and liberal locals joined forces, declared their loyalty to King Ferdinand, and formed committees (*juntas*). Between May of 1810 and July of 1811, the *juntas* in Argentina, Chile, Paraguay, Venezuela, Bolivia, and Colombia all declared independence. Fighting erupted between Spanish authorities in Latin America and the members and followers of the *juntas*. In Mexico City another *junta* declared loyalty to King Ferdinand and independence.

Society in Latin America was sharply distinguished according to race and the purity of Spanish blood. **Miguel Hidalgo**, a 60-year-old priest and enlightened intellectual, disregarded the racial distinctions of the society. He had been fighting for the interests of the Indians and part Indian/part white citizens of Mexico, including a call for the return of land stolen from the Indians. He called for an uprising in 1810.

Simon Bolivar had been born into Venezuela's wealthy society and educated in Europe. With Francisco de Miranda, he declared Venezuela and Columbia to be republics and removed all Spanish trading restrictions. These leaders also removed taxes on the sale of food, ended payment of tribute to the government by the local Indians, and prohibited slavery. In March 1812 Caracas was devastated by an earthquake. When the Spanish clergy in Caracas proclaimed the earthquake God's act of vengeance against the rebel government, they then provided support for the Spanish government officials, who quickly regained control.

When Ferdinand was returned to power in 1814, it was no longer possible for the rebel groups to claim to act in his name. Bolivar was driven to Colombia, where he gathered a small army that returned to Venezuela in 1817. As his army grew, Spain became concerned, and the military moved into the interior of Venezuela. This action aroused the local people to active rebellion. As he freed slaves, Bolivar gained support and strength. Realizing that he did not have the strength to take Caracas, he moved his people to Colombia. Bolivar's forces defeated the Spanish and organized "Gran Colombia" (which included present-day Ecuador, Colombia and Panama), and he became president in 1819. When Ferdinand encountered difficulties in Spain, the soldiers assembled to be transported to the Americas revolted. Several groups in Spain joined the revolt and together, drove Ferdinand from power. Bolivar took advantage of the opportunity and took his army back into Venezuela. In 1821, Bolivar defeated the Spanish, took Caracas, and established Venezuelan freedom from Spanish rule.

In Peru, **San Martin** took his force into Lima amid celebration. Bolivar provided assistance in winning Peru's independence in 1822. Bolivar now controlled Peru. By 1824, Bolivar had combined forces with local groups and rid South America of Spanish control.

In 1807, Queen Maria of Portugal fled to escape Napoleon. The royal family sailed to Brazil, where they were welcomed by the local people. Rio de Janeiro became the temporary capital of Portugal's empire. Maria's son Joao ruled as regent. He opened Brazil's trade with other nations; gave the British favorable tax rates in gratitude for their assistance against Napoleon; and opened Brazil to foreign scholars, visitors and immigrants. In 1815, he made Brazil a kingdom that was united with Portugal. By 1817 there was economic trouble in Brazil along with unrest over repression (such as censorship). This discontent became a rebellion that was repressed by Joao's military.

When Napoleon's forces withdrew from Portugal, the British asked Joao to return. Liberals took power in Portugal and in Spain and both drafted liberal constitutions. By 1821, Joao decided to return to Portugal as a constitutional monarch. He left his oldest son Pedro on the throne in Brazil. When Portugal tried to reinstate economic advantages for Portugal and restrict Brazil, resistance began to grow. Pedro did not want to be controlled by Portugal and was labeled a rebel. When he learned that Portuguese troops had been sent to arrest him, he prohibited the landing of the ship, sent it back to Portugal, and declared independence in 1922. In a little more than a month he was declared Emperor of Brazil.

Until the early years of the twentieth century Russia was ruled by a succession of Czars. The Czars ruled as autocrats or, sometimes, despots. Society was essentially feudalistic and was structured in three levels. The top level was held by the Czar. The second level was composed of the rich nobles who held government positions and owned vast tracts of land. The third level of the society was composed of the remaining people, who lived in poverty as peasants or serfs.

There was discontent among the peasants. There were several unsuccessful attempts to rebel during the nineteenth century, but they were quickly suppressed. The **Russian Revolutions** of 1905 and 1917, however, were quite different.

The causes of the 1905 Revolution were:

- Discontent with the social structure
- Discontent with the living conditions of the peasants
- Discontent with working conditions despite industrialization
- General discontent aggravated by the Russo-Japanese War (1904-1905) with inflation and rising prices. Peasants who had been able to eke out a living began to starve.
- Many fighting troops killed in battles as Russia lost a war to Japan (Russo-Japanese War) because of poor leadership, lack of training, and inferior weaponry
- Czar Nicholas II refused to end the war despite setbacks.
- In January 1905 Port Arthur fell.

A trade union leader, Father Gapon, organized a protest to demand an end to the war, industrial reform, more civil liberties, and a constituent assembly. Over 150,000 peasants joined a demonstration outside the Czar's Winter Palace. Before the demonstrators even spoke, the palace guard opened fire on the crowd. This destroyed the people's trust in the Czar. Illegal trade unions and political parties formed and organized strikes to gain power.

The strikes eventually brought the Russian economy to a halt. This led Czar Nicholas II to sign the October Manifesto, which created a constitutional monarchy, extended some civil rights, and gave the Parliament limited legislative power. In a very short period of time, the Czar disbanded the Parliament and violated the promised civil liberties. This violation further stirred discontent and rebellion.

Causes of the 1917 Revolution were:

- The violation of the October Manifesto
- Defeats on the battlefields during WWI caused discontent, loss of life, and a popular desire to withdraw from the war.
- The Czar continued to appoint unqualified people to government posts and handle the country with general incompetence.
- The Czar also listened to his wife's (Alexandra) advice. She was strongly influenced by Rasputin. This caused increased discontent among all level of the social structure.
- WWI had caused another surge in prices and scarcity of many items. Most of the peasants could not afford to buy bread.

Workers in Petrograd went on strike in 1917 over the need for food. The Czar again ordered troops to suppress the strike. This time, however, the troops sided with the workers. The revolution then took a unique direction. The Parliament created a provisional government to rule the country. The military and the workers also created their own governments, called soviets (popularly elected local councils). The Parliament was composed of nobles, who soon lost control of the country when they failed to comply with the wishes of the populace. The result was chaos.

The political leaders who had previously been driven into exile returned. Lenin, Stalin, and Trotsky won the support of the peasants with the promise of "Peace, Land, and Bread." The Parliament, on the other hand, continued the country's involvement in the war. Lenin and the Bolshevik Party gained the support of the Red Guard and together overthrew the provisional government. In short order, they had complete control of Russia and established a new communist state.

The most significant differences between the 1905 and 1917 revolutions were the 1) formation of political parties and their use of propaganda, and 2) the support of the military and some of the nobles in 1917.

Declaration of Independence and the Declaration of the Rights of Man.

Jean-Jacques Rousseau (1712-1778) was one of the most famous and influential political theorists before the French Revolution. His most important and most studied work is *The Social Contract* (1762). He was concerned with what should be the proper form of society and government. However, unlike Hobbes, Rousseau did not view the state of nature as one of absolute chaos. The problem as Rousseau saw it was that the natural harmony of the state of nature was due to people's intuitive goodness not to their actual reason. Reason only developed once a civilized society was established.

Rousseau's most direct influence was upon the **French Revolution** (1789-1815). The **Declaration of the Rights of Man and of the Citizen** (1789), explicitly recognized the sovereignty of the general will as expressed in the law. In contrast to the American **Declaration of Independence**, it contains explicit mention of the obligations and duties of the citizen, such as assenting to taxes in support of the military or police forces for the common good. In modern times, ideas such as Rousseau's have often been used to justify the ideas of authoritarian and totalitarian socialist systems.

The three most basic rights guaranteed by the Declaration of Independence are "life, liberty, and the pursuit of happiness." The first one is self-explanatory: Americans are guaranteed the right to live their lives in America. The second one is basic as well: Americans are guaranteed the right to live their lives *free* in America. (This principle, however, has been violated many times, most notably with Native Americans and African-Americans.) The last basic right is more esoteric, but no less important: Americans are guaranteed the right to pursue a happy life. First and foremost, they are allowed the ability to make a life for themselves in America, "the Land of Opportunity." That happiness also extends to the pursuit of life free from oppression or discrimination, two things that, again, African-Americans, women, and non-white Americans have suffered from to varying degrees throughout the history of the country.

The Declaration of Independence is an outgrowth of both ancient Greek ideas of democracy and individual rights, and the ideas of the European Enlightenment and the Renaissance, especially the ideology of the political thinker **John Locke**. Thomas Jefferson (1743-1826), author of the Declaration, borrowed much from Locke's theories and writings. John Locke was one of the most influential political writers of the seventeenth century. He put great emphasis on human rights and put forth the belief that when governments violate those rights, people should rebel. He wrote the book "Two Treatises of Government" in 1690, which had tremendous influence on political thought in the American colonies and helped shape the U.S. Constitution and Declaration of Independence.

Essentially, Jefferson applied Locke's principles to the contemporary American situation. Jefferson argued that the currently reigning King George III had repeatedly violated the rights of the colonists as subjects of the British Crown. Disdaining the colonial petition for redress of grievances (a right guaranteed by the Declaration of Rights of 1689), the King seemed bent upon establishing an "absolute tyranny" over the colonies. Such disgraceful behavior itself violated the reasons for which government had been instituted. The American colonists were left with no choice. "It is their right, it is their duty, to throw off such a government, and to provide new guards for their future security," wrote Thomas Jefferson.

By 1776, the colonists and their representatives in the Second Continental Congress realized that things were past the point of no return. The Declaration of Independence was drafted and declared July 4, 1776. George Washington labored against tremendous odds to wage a victorious war. The turning point in the Americans' favor occurred in 1777 with the American victory at Saratoga. This victory was supported by the French decision to align itself with the Americans against the British. With the aid of Admiral de Grasse and French warships blocking the entrance to Chesapeake Bay, British General Cornwallis trapped at Yorktown, Virginia, surrendered in 1781 and the war was over. The Treaty of Paris officially ending the war was signed in 1783.

The Declaration of the Rights of Man and of the Citizen is a document created by the French National Assembly, issued in 1789. It sets forth the "natural, inalienable and sacred rights of man." It proclaims the following rights:

- Men are born and remain free and equal in rights. Social distinctions may only be founded upon the general good.
- The aim of all political association is the preservation of the natural and imprescriptible rights of man: liberty, property, security, and resistance to oppression.
- All sovereignty resides essentially in the nation. No body or individual may exercise any authority which does not proceed directly from the nation.
- Liberty is the freedom to do everything which injures no one else; hence the exercise of these rights has no limits except those which assure to the other members of the society the enjoyment of the same rights. These limits can only be determined by law.
- Law can only prohibit such actions as are hurtful to society.
- Law is the expression of the general will. Every citizen has a right to participate in the formation of law. It must be the same for all. All citizens, being equal in the eyes of the law, are equally eligible to all dignities and to all public positions and occupations, according to their abilities.
- No person shall be accused, arrested, or imprisoned except in the cases and according to the forms prescribed by law.
- The law shall provide for such punishments only as are strictly and obviously necessary.

- All persons are held innocent until they have been declared guilty. If it is necessary to arrest a person, all harshness not essential to the securing of the prisoner's person shall be severely repressed by law.
- No one shall be disquieted on account of his opinions, including religious views, provided their manifestation does not disturb the peace.
- The free communication of ideas and opinions is one of the most precious of the rights of man.
- The security of the rights of man and of the citizen requires public military force. These forces are, therefore, established for the good of all and not for the personal advantage of those to whom they shall be entrusted.
- A common contribution is essential for the maintenance of the public forces and for the cost of administration. This should be equitably distributed among all the citizens in proportion to their means.
- All the citizens have a right to decide, either personally or by their representatives, as to the necessity of the public contribution.
- Society has the right to require of every public agent an account of his administration.
- A society in which the observance of the law is not assured nor the separation of powers defined has no constitution at all.

Since property is an inviolable and sacred right, no one shall be deprived thereof except where public necessity, legally determined, shall clearly demand it, and then only on condition that the owner shall have been previously and equitably indemnified.

Skill 1.6   Analyze the causes and effects of exploration, settlement, and growth in Africa, the Americas, Asia (including the Middle East), Europe, and Oceania.

The Meeting of Three Worlds: Africa, Europe, and the Americas

The Age of Exploration actually had its beginnings centuries before exploration actually took place. The rise and spread of Islam in the seventh century and its subsequent control over the holy city of Jerusalem led to the European so-called Holy Wars, the Crusades, to free Jerusalem and the Holy Land from this control. Even though the Crusades were not a success, those who survived and returned to their homes and countries in Western Europe brought back with them new products such as silks, spices, perfumes, and new and different foods. New ideas, inventions, and methods also went to Western Europe with the returning Crusaders, and from these new influences was the intellectual stimulation which led to the period known as the Renaissance.

Colonization and Settlement (1585-1763)

The part of North America claimed by France was called New France and consisted of the land west of the Appalachian Mountains. This area of claims and settlement included the St. Lawrence Valley, the Great Lakes, the Mississippi Valley, and the entire region of land westward to the Rocky Mountains. They established the permanent settlements of Montreal and New Orleans, thus giving them control of the two major gateways into the heart of North America, the vast, rich interior. The St. Lawrence River, the Great Lakes, and the Mississippi River along with its tributaries made it possible for the French explorers and traders to roam at will, virtually unhindered in exploring, trapping, trading, and furthering the interests of France.

Most of the French settlements were in Canada along the St. Lawrence River. Only scattered forts and trading posts were found in the upper Mississippi Valley and Great Lakes region. The rulers of France originally intended New France to have vast estates owned by nobles and worked by peasants who would live on the estates in compact farming villages—the New World version of the Old World's medieval system of feudalism. However, it didn't work out that way. Each of the nobles wanted his estate to be on the river for ease of transportation. The peasants working the estates wanted the prime waterfront location, also. The result of all this real estate squabbling was that New France's settled areas wound up mostly as a string of farmhouses stretching from Quebec to Montreal along the St. Lawrence and Richelieu Rivers.

In the non-settled areas in the interior were the French fur traders. They made friends with the friendly tribes of Indians, spending the winters with them getting the furs needed for trade. In the spring, they would return to Montreal in time to take advantage of trading their furs for the products brought by the cargo ships from France, which usually arrived at about the same time. Most of the wealth for New France and its "Mother Country" was from the fur trade, which provided a livelihood for many, many people. Manufacturers and workmen back in France, ship-owners and merchants, as well as the fur traders and their Indian allies all benefited. However, the freedom of roaming and trapping in the interior was a strong enticement for the younger, stronger men and resulted in the French not strengthening the areas settled along the St. Lawrence.

Into the eighteenth century, the rivalry with the British was growing stronger and stronger. New France was united under a single government and enjoyed the support of many Indian allies. The French traders were very diligent in not destroying the forests and driving away game upon which the Indians depended for life. It was difficult for the French to defend all of their settlements as they were scattered over half of the continent. However, by the early 1750s, in Western Europe, France was the most powerful nation. Its armies were superior to all others and its navy was giving the British stiff competition for control of the seas. The stage was set for confrontation in both Europe and America.

Spanish settlement had its beginnings in the Caribbean with the establishment of colonies on Hispaniola (at Santo Domingo which became the capital of the West Indies), Puerto Rico, and Cuba. There were a number of reasons for Spanish involvement in the Americas, to name just a few:

- spirit of adventure
- desire for land
- expansion of Spanish power, influence, and empire
- desire for great wealth
- expansion of Roman Catholic influence and conversion of native peoples

The first permanent settlement in what is now the United States was in 1565 at St. Augustine, Florida. A later permanent settlement in the southwestern United States was in 1609 at Santa Fe, New Mexico. At the peak of Spanish power, the area in the United States claimed, settled, and controlled by Spain included Florida and all land west of the Mississippi River—quite a piece of choice real estate. Of course, France and England also lay claim to the same areas. Nonetheless, ranches and missions were built, and the Indians who came in contact with the Spaniards were introduced to animals, plants, and seeds from the Old World that they had never seen before. Animals brought in included horses, cattle, donkeys, pigs, sheep, goats, and poultry.

Barrels were cut in half and filled with earth to transport and transplant trees bearing apples, oranges, limes, cherries, pears, walnuts, olives, lemons, figs, apricots, almonds

Even sugar cane and flowers made it to America along with bags of seeds of wheat, barley, rye, flax, lentils, rice, and peas.

All Spanish colonies belonged to the King of Spain. He was considered an absolute monarch with complete or absolute power and claimed rule by divine right, the belief being God had given him the right to rule, and he answered only to God for his actions. His word was final and the law. The people had no voice in government. The land, the people, the wealth all belonged to him to use as he pleased. He appointed personal representatives or viceroys to rule for him in his colonies. They ruled in his name with complete authority. Since the majority of them were friends and advisers, they were richly rewarded with land grants, gold and silver, privileges of trading, and the right to operate the gold and silver mines.

For the needed labor in the mines and on the plantations, Indians were used first as slaves. However, they either rapidly died out due to a lack of immunity from European diseases or escaped into nearby jungles or mountains. As a result, African slaves were brought in, especially to the islands of the West Indies. Some historians state that Latin American slavery was less harsh than in the later English colonies in North America. Three reasons for this are:

- The following of a slave code based on ancient Roman laws;
- The efforts of the Roman Catholic Church to protect and defend slaves because of efforts to convert them;
- The existence of less prejudice because of racial mixtures in parts of Spain controlled at one time by dark-skinned Moors from North Africa.

Regardless, slavery was still slavery and was very harsh—cruelly denying dignity and human worth and leading to desperate resistance.

Spain's control over her New World colonies lasted more than 300 years, longer than England or France. To this day, Spanish influence remains in names of places, art, architecture, music, literature, law, and cuisine. The Spanish settlements in North America were not commercial enterprises but were for protection and defense of the trading and wealth from their colonies in Mexico and South America. The Russians hunted seals along the Pacific coast; the English moved into Florida and into the Appalachians; and the French traders and trappers made their way from Louisiana and other parts of New France into Spanish territory. The Spanish never realized or understood that self-sustaining economic development and colonial trade were so important. Consequently, the Spanish settlements in the U.S. never really prospered.

The treasure and wealth found in Spanish New World colonies went back to Spain to be used to buy whatever goods and products were needed instead of setting up industries to make what was needed. As the amount of gold and silver was depleted, Spain could not pay for the goods needed and was unable to produce goods for themselves. Also, at the same time, Spanish treasure ships at sea were being seized by English and Dutch "pirates" taking the wealth to the coffers of their own countries.

Before 1763, England was rapidly becoming the most powerful of the three major Western European powers. Its thirteen colonies, located between the Atlantic and the Appalachians, physically occupied the least amount of land. Moreover, it is interesting that even before the Spanish Armada was defeated, two Englishmen, Sir Humphrey Gilbert and his half-brother Sir Walter Raleigh, were unsuccessful in their attempts to build successful permanent colonies in the New World. Nonetheless, the thirteen English colonies were successful, and by the time they had gained their independence from Britain, they were more than able to govern themselves. They had a rich historical heritage of law, tradition, and documents leading the way to constitutional government conducted according to laws and customs. The settlers in the British colonies highly valued individual freedom, democratic government, and getting ahead through hard work.

Skill 1.7 **Identify individuals, ideas, and events that have influenced economic, cultural, social, and political institutions in the United States.**

The **War for Independence** occurred due to a number of changes, the two most important ones being economic and political. By the end of the French and Indian War in 1763, Britain's American colonies were thirteen out of a total of 33 scattered around the earth. Like all other countries, Britain strove for having a strong economy and a favorable balance of trade. To have that delicate balance a nation needs wealth, self-sufficiency, and a powerful army and navy. The overseas colonies would provide raw materials for the industries in the Mother Country, be a market for the finished products by buying them and assist the Mother Country in becoming powerful and strong (as in the case of Great Britain). By having a strong merchant fleet, it would be a school for training the Royal Navy and provide bases of operation for the Royal Navy.

So between 1607 and 1763, at various times for various reasons, the British Parliament enacted different laws to assist the government in getting and keeping this trade balance. One series of laws required that most of the manufacturing be done only in England and prohibited exporting any wool or woolen cloth from the colonies as well as the manufacture of beaver hats or iron products. The colonists weren't particularly concerned as they had no money and no highly skilled labor to set up any industries anyway.

The **Navigation Acts** of 1651 put restrictions on shipping and trade within the British Empire, requiring that it was allowed only on British ships. This increased the strength of the British merchant fleet and greatly benefited the American colonists. Since they were British citizens, they could have their own vessels, building and operating them as well. By the end of the war in 1763, the shipyards in the colonies were building one-third of the merchant ships under the British flag. There were quite a number of wealthy, colonial merchants.

The Navigation Act of 1660 restricted the shipment and sale of colonial products to England only. In 1663 another Navigation Act stipulated that the colonies had to buy manufactured products only from England and that any European goods going to the colonies had to go to England first. These acts were a protection from enemy ships and pirates—and from competition from European rivals.

The New England and Middle Atlantic colonies at first felt threatened by these laws as they had started producing many of the products being produced in Britain. They soon found new markets for their goods and began what was known as a **triangular trade**. Colonial vessels started the first part of the triangle by sailing for Africa loaded with kegs of rum from colonial distilleries. On Africa's West Coast, the rum was traded for either gold or slaves. The second part of the triangle was from Africa to the West Indies where slaves were traded for molasses, sugar, or money. The third part of the triangle was home, bringing home sugar or molasses (to make more rum), gold, and silver.

The major concern of the British government was that the trade violated the 1733 Molasses Act. Planters had wanted the colonists to buy all of their molasses in the British West Indies, but these islands could give the traders only about one-eighth of the amount of molasses needed for distilling the rum. The colonists were forced to buy the rest of what they needed from the French, Dutch, and Spanish islands, thus evading the law by not paying the high duty on the molasses bought from these islands. If Britain had enforced the Molasses Act, economic and financial chaos and ruin would have occurred. Nevertheless, for this Act and all the other mercantile laws, the government followed the policy of "salutary neglect," deliberately failing to enforce the laws.

In 1763, after the war, money was needed to pay the British war debt, for the defense of the empire, and to pay for the governing of 33 colonies scattered around the earth. It was decided to adopt a new colonial policy and pass laws to raise revenue. It was reasoned that the colonists were subjects of the king and since the king and his ministers had spent a great deal of money defending and protecting them (this especially for the American colonists), it was only right and fair that the colonists should help pay the costs of their defense. The earlier laws passed had been for the purposes of regulating production and trade which generally put money into colonial pockets. These new laws would take some of that rather hard-earned money out of their pockets, and it would be done, in colonial eyes, unjustly and illegally.

Before 1763, except for trade and supplying raw materials, the colonies had been left pretty much to themselves. England looked on the colonies merely as part of an economic or commercial empire. Little consideration was given as to how they were to conduct their daily affairs, so the colonists became very independent, self-reliant, and extremely skillful at handling those daily affairs. This, in turn, gave rise to leadership, initiative, achievement, and vast experience. In fact, there was a far greater degree of independence and self-government in the British colonies in America than could be found in Britain or the major countries on the Continent or any other colonies anywhere. There were a number of reasons for this:

1. The religious and scriptural teachings of previous centuries put forth the worth of the individual and equality in God's sight. Keep in mind that freedom of worship and from religious persecution were major reasons to live in the New World.

2. European Protestants, especially Calvinists, believed and taught the idea that government originates from those governed, that rulers are required to protect individual rights, and that the governed have the right and privilege to choose their rulers.

3. Trading companies put into practice the principle that their members had the right to make the decisions and shape the policies affecting their lives.

4. The colonists believed and supported the idea that a person's property should not be taken without his consent, based on that treasured English document, the Magna Carta, and English common law.

5. From about 1700 to 1750, population increases in America came about through immigration and generations of descendants of the original settlers. The immigrants were mainly Scots-Irish who hated the English, Germans who cared nothing about England, and black slaves who knew nothing about England. The descendants of many of the original settlers had never been out of America at any time.

6. In America, as new towns and counties were formed, there began the practice of representation in government. Representatives to the colonial legislative assemblies were elected from the district in which they lived, chosen by qualified property-owning male voters, and represented the interests of the political district from which they were elected. However, each of the thirteen colonies had a royal governor appointed by the king representing *his* interests in the colonies. Nevertheless, the colonial legislative assemblies controlled the purse strings, having the power to vote on all issues involving money to be spent by the colonial governments.

Thomas Paine (1737-1809), the great American political theorist, wrote: "These are the times that try men's souls" in his 16-part pamphlet *The Crisis*. Paine's authoring of *Common Sense* was an important step in spreading information to the American colonists about their need for independence from Great Britain.

Contrary to this was the governmental set up in England. Members of Parliament were not elected to represent their own districts. They were considered representative of classes, not individuals. If some members of a professional or commercial class or some landed interests were able to elect representatives, then those classes or special interests were represented. It had nothing at all to do with numbers or territories. Some large population centers had no direct representation at all, yet the people there considered themselves represented by men elected from their particular class or interest somewhere else. Consequently, it was extremely difficult for the English to understand why the American merchants and landowners claimed they were not represented because they themselves did not vote for a member of Parliament.

The colonists' protest of "no taxation without representation" was meaningless to the English. Parliament represented the entire nation, was completely unlimited in legislation, and had become supreme; and the colonists were incensed at the English attitude of "of course you have representation—everyone does." The colonists considered their colonial legislative assemblies equal to Parliament, totally unacceptable in England, of course. There were two different environments: the older traditional British system in the "mother country" and new ideas and different ways of doing things in America. In a new country, a new environment has little or no tradition, institutions, or vested interests. New ideas and traditions grew extremely fast pushing aside what was left of the old ideas and old traditions. By 1763, Britain had changed its perception of its American colonies to their being a "territorial" empire. The stage was set and the conditions right for a showdown.

In 1763, Parliament decided to have a standing army in North America to reinforce British control. In 1765, the **Quartering Act** was passed requiring the colonists to provide supplies and living quarters for the British troops. In addition, efforts by the British were made to keep the peace by establishing good relations with the Indians. Consequently, a proclamation was issued which prohibited any American colonists from making any settlements west of the Appalachians until provided for through treaties with the Indians.

The Sugar Act of 1764 required efficient collection of taxes on any molasses brought into the colonies. The Act also gave British officials free license to conduct searches of the premises of anyone suspected of violating the law. The colonists were taxed on newspapers, legal documents, and other printed matter under the **Stamp Act of 1765**. Although a stamp tax was already in use in England, the colonists would have none of it, and after the ensuing uproar of rioting and mob violence, Parliament repealed the tax.

Of course, great exultation, jubilance, and wild joy resulted when news of the repeal reached America. However, what the celebrators did not notice was the small, quiet Declaratory Act attached to the repeal. This Act plainly and unequivocally stated that Parliament still had the right to make all laws for the colonies. It denied their right to be taxed only by their own colonial legislatures—a very crucial, important piece of legislation. Other acts leading up to armed conflict included the **Townshend Acts** passed in 1767 taxing lead, paint, paper, and tea brought into the colonies. This increased anger and tension resulting in the British sending troops to New York City and Boston.

In Boston, mob violence provoked retaliation by the troops thus bringing about the deaths of five people and the wounding of eight others. The so-called Boston Massacre shocked Americans and British alike. Subsequently, in 1770, Parliament voted to repeal all the provisions of the Townshend Acts with the exception of the tea tax. In 1773, the tax on tea sold by the British East India Company was substantially reduced, fueling colonial anger once more. This gave the company an unfair trade advantage and forcibly reminded the colonists of the British right to tax them. Merchants refused to sell the tea; colonists refused to buy and drink it; and a shipload of it was dumped into Boston Harbor—the Boston Tea Party.

In 1774, the passage of the Quebec Act extended the limits of that Canadian colony's boundary southward to include territory located north of the Ohio River. However, the punishment for Boston's Tea Party came in the same year with the Intolerable Acts. Boston's port was closed; the royal governor of the colony of Massachusetts was given increased power, and the colonists were compelled to house and feed the British soldiers. The propaganda activities of the patriot organizations **Sons of Liberty** and **Committees of Correspondence** kept the opposition and resistance before everyone. Delegates from twelve colonies met in Philadelphia September 5, 1774, in the First Continental Congress. They opposed acts of lawlessness and wanted some form of peaceful settlement with Britain. They maintained American loyalty to the mother country and affirmed Parliament's power over colonial foreign affairs.

They insisted on repeal of the **Intolerable Acts** and demanded ending all trade with Britain until this took place. The reply from King George III, the last king of America, was an insistence of colonial submission to British rule—or be crushed. With the start of the Revolutionary War April 19, 1775, the Second Continental Congress began meeting in Philadelphia May 10th that year to conduct the business of war and government for the next six years.

The British had been extremely lax and totally inconsistent in enforcement of the mercantile or trade laws passed in the years before 1754. The government itself was not particularly stable, so actions against the colonies occurred in anger with an attitude of moral superiority, that they knew how to manage America better than the Americans did themselves. Of course, this points to a lack of sufficient knowledge of conditions and opinions in America. The colonists had been left on their own for nearly 150 years, and by the time the Revolutionary War began, they were quite adept at self-government and adequately handling the affairs of their daily lives. The Americans equated ownership of land or property with the right to vote. Property was considered the foundation of life and liberty, and in the colonial mind and tradition, these went together.

Therefore when an indirect tax on tea was made, the British felt that since it wasn't a direct tax, there should be no objection to it. The colonists viewed any tax, direct or indirect, as an attack on their property. They felt that as a representative body, the British Parliament should protect British citizens, including the colonists, from arbitrary taxation. Since they felt they were not represented, Parliament, in their eyes, gave them no protection. So, war began. August 23, 1775, George III declared that the colonies were in rebellion and warned them to stop.

By 1776, the colonists and their representatives in the Second Continental Congress realized that things were past the point of no return. The Declaration of Independence was drafted and declared July 4, 1776. George Washington labored against tremendous odds to wage a victorious war. The turning point in the Americans' favor occurred in 1777 with the American victory at **Saratoga**. This victory decided the French to align themselves with the Americans against the British. With the aid of Admiral de Grasse and French warships blocking the entrance to Chesapeake Bay, British General Cornwallis, trapped at Yorktown, Virginia, surrendered in 1781, and the war was over. The Treaty of Paris officially ending the war was signed in 1783.

During the war, and after independence was declared, the former colonies now found themselves independent states. The Second Continental Congress was conducting a war with representation by delegates from thirteen separate states. The Congress had no power to act for the states or to require them to accept and follow its wishes. A permanent united government was needed. On November 15, 1777, the Articles of Confederation were adopted, creating a league of free and independent states.

The slavery issue flared again not to be done away with until the end of the Civil War. It was obvious that newly acquired territory would be divided up into territories and later become states. Factions of Northerners advocated prohibition of slavery and Southerners favored slavery. A third faction arose supporting the doctrine of **popular sovereignty** which stated that people living in territories and states should be allowed to decide for themselves whether or not slavery should be permitted. In 1849, California applied for admittance to the Union and the furor began.

The result was the **Compromise of 1850**, a series of laws designed as a final solution to the issue. Concessions made to the North included the admission of California as a free state and the abolition of slave trading in Washington, D.C. The laws also provided for the creation of the New Mexico and Utah territories. As a concession to Southerners, the residents there would decide whether to permit slavery when these two territories became states. In addition, Congress authorized implementation of stricter measures to capture runaway slaves.

A few years later, Congress took up consideration of new territories between Missouri and present-day Idaho. Again, heated debate over permitting slavery in these areas flared up. Those opposed to slavery used the **Missouri Compromise** to prove their point showing that the land being considered for territories was part of the area the Compromise had been designated as banned to slavery. On May 25, 1854, Congress passed the infamous **Kansas-Nebraska Act** which nullified the provision creating the territories of Kansas and Nebraska. This provided for the people of these two territories to decide for themselves whether or not to permit slavery to exist there. Feelings were so deep and divided that any further attempts to compromise would meet with little, if any, success. Political and social turmoil swirled everywhere. Kansas was called "Bleeding Kansas" because of the extreme violence and bloodshed throughout the territory because two governments existed there, one pro-slavery and the other anti-slavery.

The Supreme Court decided that residing in a free state and free territory did not make Scott a free man because Scott (and all other slaves) was not an U.S. citizen or a state citizen of Missouri. Therefore, he did not have the right to sue in state or federal courts. The Court went a step further and ruled that the old Missouri Compromise was now unconstitutional because Congress did not have the power to prohibit slavery in the Territories.

It is ironic that South Carolina was the first state to secede from the Union and the first shots of the war were fired on Fort Sumter in Charleston Harbor. Both sides quickly prepared for war. The North had more in its favor: a larger population; superiority in finances and transportation facilities; manufacturing, agricultural, and natural resources. The North possessed most of the nation's gold, had about 92% of all industries, and almost all known supplies of copper, coal, iron, and various other minerals. Most of the nation's railroads were in the North and mid-West, men and supplies could be moved wherever needed; food could be transported from the farms of the mid-West to workers in the East and to soldiers on the battlefields. Trade with nations overseas could go on as usual due to control of the navy and the merchant fleet. The Northern states numbered 24 and included western (California and Oregon) and border (Maryland, Delaware, Kentucky, Missouri, and West Virginia) states.

The Southern states numbered eleven and included South Carolina, Georgia, Florida, Alabama, Mississippi, Louisiana, Texas, Virginia, North Carolina, Tennessee, and Arkansas, making up the Confederacy. Although outnumbered in population, the South was completely confident of victory. They knew that all they had to do was fight a defensive war and protect their own territory. The North had to invade and defeat an area almost the size of Western Europe. They figured the North would tire of the struggle and gave up. Another advantage of the South was that a number of its best officers had graduated from the U.S. Military Academy at West Point and had had long years of army experience. Many had exercised varying degrees of command in the Indian Wars and the war with Mexico. Men from the South were conditioned to living outdoors and were more familiar with horses and firearms than men from northeastern cities. Since cotton was such an important crop, Southerners felt that British and French textile mills were so dependent on raw cotton that they would be forced to help the Confederacy in the war.

The South had specific reasons and goals for fighting the war, more so than the North. The major aim of the Confederacy never wavered: to win independence, the right to govern themselves as they wished, and to preserve slavery. The Northerners were not as clear in their reasons for conducting war. At the beginning, most believed, along with Lincoln, that preservation of the Union was paramount. Only a few extremely fanatical abolitionists looked on the war as a way to end slavery. However, by war's end, more and more northerners had come to believe that freeing the slaves was just as important as restoring the Union.

The war strategies for both sides were relatively clear and simple. The South planned a defensive war, wearing down the North until it agreed to peace on Southern terms. One exception was to gain control of Washington, D.C., go north through the Shenandoah Valley into Maryland and Pennsylvania and drive a wedge between the Northeast and mid-West, interrupt the lines of communication, and end the war quickly. The North had three basic strategies:

1. Blockade the Confederate coastline in order to cripple the South;

2. Seize control of the Mississippi River and interior railroad lines to split the Confederacy in two; and

3. Seize the Confederate capital of Richmond, Virginia, driving southward joining up with Union forces coming east from the Mississippi Valley.

The South won decisively until the Battle of Gettysburg, July 1 - 3, 1863. Until Gettysburg, Lincoln's commanders, McDowell and McClellan, were less than desirable; Burnside and Hooker, not what was needed. Lee, on the other hand, had many able officers; he depended heavily on Jackson and Stuart. Jackson died at Chancellorsville and was replaced by Longstreet. Lee decided to invade the North and depended on J.E.B. Stuart and his cavalry to keep him informed of the location of Union troops and their strengths. Four things worked against Lee at Gettysburg:

1. The Union troops gained the best positions and the best ground first, making it easier to make a stand there.

2. Lee's move into Northern territory put him and his army a long way from food and supply lines. They were more or less on their own.

3. Lee thought that his Army of Northern Virginia was invincible and could fight and win under any conditions or circumstances.

4. Stuart and his men did not arrive at Gettysburg until the end of the second day of fighting, and by then, it was too little too late. He and the men had had to detour around Union soldiers, and he was delayed getting the information Lee needed.

Consequently, he made the mistake of failing to listen to Longstreet and following the strategy of regrouping back into Southern territory to the supply lines. Lee felt that regrouping was retreating and almost an admission of defeat. He was convinced the army would be victorious. Longstreet was concerned about the Union troops occupying the best positions and felt that regrouping to a better position would be an advantage. He was also concerned about the distance from supply lines.

It was not the intention of either side to fight there, but the fighting began when a Confederate brigade stumbled into a unit of Union cavalry while looking for shoes. The third and last day Lee launched the final attempt to break Union lines. General George Pickett sent his division of three brigades under Generals Garnet, Kemper, and Armistead against Union troops on Cemetery Ridge under command of General Winfield Scott Hancock. Union lines held, and Lee and the defeated Army of Northern Virginia made their way back to Virginia. Although Lincoln's commander George Meade successfully turned back a Confederate charge, he and the Union troops failed to pursue Lee and the Confederates. Yet, this battle was the turning point for the North. After this, Lee never again had the troop strength to launch a major offensive.

The day after Gettysburg, on July 4, Vicksburg, Mississippi, surrendered to Union General Ulysses Grant, thus severing the western Confederacy from the eastern part. In September 1863, the Confederacy won its last important victory at Chickamauga. In November, the Union victory at Chattanooga made it possible for Union troops to go into Alabama and Georgia, splitting the eastern Confederacy in two. Lincoln gave Grant command of all Northern armies in March of 1864. Grant led his armies into battles in Virginia while Phil Sheridan and his cavalry did as much damage as possible. In a skirmish at a place called Yellow Tavern, Virginia, Sheridan's and Stuart's forces met, with Stuart being fatally wounded. The Union won the Battle of Mobile Bay and in May 1864, William Tecumseh Sherman began his march to successfully demolish Atlanta, then on to Savannah. He and his troops turned northward through the Carolinas to Grant in Virginia. On April 9, 1865, Lee formally surrendered to Grant at Appomattox Courthouse, Virginia.

The Civil War took more American lives than any other war in history, the South losing one-third of its soldiers in battle compared to about one-sixth for the North. More than half of the deaths were caused by disease and the horrendous conditions of field hospitals. Both sides paid a tremendous economic price, but the South suffered more severely from direct damages. Destruction was pervasive with towns, farms, trade, industry, lives, and homes of men, women, and children all destroyed and an entire Southern way of life lost. The deep resentment, bitterness, and hatred that remained for generations gradually lessened as the years went by, but legacies of it surface and remain to this day.

The South had no voice in the political, social, and cultural affairs of the nation, lessening to a great degree the influence of the more traditional Southern ideals. The Northern Yankee Protestant ideals of hard work, education, and economic freedom became the standard of the United States and helped influence the development of the nation into a modern, industrial power.

The effects of the Civil War were tremendous. It changed the methods of waging war and has been called the first modern war. It introduced weapons and tactics that, when improved later, were used extensively in wars of the late 1800s and 1900s. Civil War soldiers were the first to fight in trenches, first to fight under a unified command, first to wage a defense called "major cordon defense," a strategy of advance on all fronts. They were also the first to use repeating and breech-loading weapons. Observation balloons were first used during the war along with submarines, ironclad ships, and mines. Telegraphy and railroads were put to use first in the Civil War. It was considered a modern war because of the vast destruction and was "total war," involving the use of all resources of the opposing sides. Perhaps it could not have ended other than the total defeat and unconditional surrender of one side or the other.

By executive proclamation and constitutional amendment, slavery was officially and finally ended. There remained deep prejudice and racism, which still raises its ugly head today. But the Union was preserved, and the states were finally truly united. Sectionalism, especially in the area of politics, remained strong for another 100 years but not to the degree and with the violence as existed before 1861. It has been noted that the Civil War may have been American democracy's greatest failure because from 1861 to 1865, calm reason—basic to democracy—fell to human passion. Yet, democracy did survive. The victory of the North established that no state has the right to end or leave the Union. Because of unity, the U.S. became a major global power. Lincoln never proposed to punish the South. He was most concerned with restoring the South to the Union in a program that was flexible and practical rather than rigid and unbending. He did not feel that the states had succeeded in leaving the Union but that they had left the 'family circle" for a short time. His plans consisted of two major steps:

- o All Southerners taking an oath of allegiance to the Union promising to accept all federal laws and proclamations dealing with slavery would receive a full pardon. The exceptions were men who had resigned from civil and military positions in the federal government to serve in the Confederacy, those who were part of the Confederate government, those in the Confederate army above the rank of lieutenant, and Confederates who were guilty of mistreating prisoners of war and blacks.

- o A state would be able to write a new constitution, elect new officials, and return to the Union fully equal to all other states on certain conditions. First, a minimum number of persons (at least 10% of those who were qualified voters in their states before secession from the Union who had voted in the 1860 election) must take an oath of allegiance.

As the war dragged on to its bloody, destructive conclusion, Lincoln was eager to get the states restored to the Union. He showed flexibility in his thinking as he made changes to his Reconstruction program to make it as easy and painless as possible. Of course, Congress had final approval of many actions, and it would be interesting to know how differently things might have turned out if Lincoln had lived to see some or all of his benevolent policies, supported by fellow moderates, put into action. Unfortunately, it didn't turn out that way. After Andrew Johnson became President and the Radical Republicans gained control of Congress, the harsh measures of radical Reconstruction were implemented.

The economic and social chaos in the South after the war was unbelievable with starvation and disease rampant, especially in the cities. The U.S. Army provided some relief of food and clothing for both white and blacks, but the major responsibility fell to the Freedmen's Bureau. Though the bureau agents to a certain extent helped southern whites, their main responsibility was to the freed slaves. They were to assist the freed slaves to become self-supporting and to protect them from being taken advantage of by others. Northerners looked on it as a real, honest effort to help the South out of the chaos it was in. Most white Southerners charged the Bureau with causing racial friction, deliberately encouraging the freed slaves to consider former owners as enemies.

As a result, as southern leaders began to be able to restore life as it had once been, they adopted a set of laws known as "Black Codes," containing many of the provisions of the prewar "slave codes." There were certain improvements in the lives of freed slaves, but the codes denied basic civil rights. In short, except for the condition of freedom and a few civil rights, white Southerners made every effort to keep the freed slaves in a way of life subordinate to theirs.

Radicals in Congress pointed out these illegal actions by white Southerners as evidence that they were unwilling to recognize, accept, and support the complete freedom of black Americans and could not be trusted. Therefore, Congress drafted its own program of Reconstruction, including laws that would protect and further the rights of blacks. Three amendments were added to the Constitution: the Thirteenth Amendment of 1865 outlawed slavery throughout the entire United States. The Fourteenth Amendment of 1868 made blacks American citizens. The Fifteenth Amendment of 1870 gave black Americans the right to vote and made it illegal to deny anyone the right to vote based on race.

Federal troops stationed throughout the South protected Republicans who took control of Southern governments. Bitterly resentful, many white Southerners fought the new political system by joining a secret society called the Ku Klux Klan, using violence to keep black Americans from voting and getting equality. Between 1866 and 1870, all of the states had returned to the Union, but Northern interest in Reconstruction was fading. Reconstruction officially ended when the last Federal troops left the South in 1877. It can be said that Reconstruction had a limited success as it set up public school systems and expanded legal rights of black Americans. Nevertheless, white supremacy came to be in control again, and its bitter fruitage remains.

Lincoln and Johnson had considered the conflict of Civil War as a "rebellion of individuals," but Congressional Radicals, such as Charles Sumner in the Senate, considered the Southern states as complete political organizations. He considered them in the same position as any unorganized Territory and believed they should be treated as such. Radical House leader Thaddeus Stevens considered the Confederate states not as Territories but as conquered provinces and felt they should be treated that way. President Johnson refused to work with congressional moderates, insisting on having his own way. As a result, the Radicals gained control of both houses of Congress, and when Johnson opposed their harsh measures, they came within one vote of impeaching him.

General Grant was elected President in 1868, serving two scandal-ridden terms. He was an honest, upright person, but he greatly lacked political experience—and his greatest weakness was a blind loyalty to his friends. He absolutely refused to believe that his friends were not honest and stubbornly would not admit to their using him to further their own interests. One of the sad results of the war was the rapid growth of business and industry with large corporations controlled by unscrupulous men. However, after 1877, some degree of normalcy returned and there was time for rebuilding, expansion, and growth.

Plans for Reconstruction versus its actual implementation

Following the Civil War, the nation was faced with repairing the torn Union and readmitting the Confederate states. **Reconstruction** refers to this period between 1865 and 1877 when the federal and state governments debated and implemented plans to provide civil rights to freed slaves and to set the terms under which the former Confederate states might once again join the Union.

Planning for Reconstruction began early in the war, in 1861. Abraham Lincoln's Republican Party in Washington favored the extension of voting rights to black men but was divided as to how far to extend the right. Moderates, such as Lincoln, wanted only literate blacks and those who had fought for the Union to be allowed to vote. Radical Republicans wanted to extend the vote to all black men. Conservative Democrats did not want to give black men the vote at all. In the case of former Confederate soldiers, moderates wanted to allow all but former leaders to vote while the Radicals wanted to require an oath from all eligible voters that they had never borne arms against the U.S., which would have excluded all former rebels. On the issue of readmission into the Union, moderates favored a much lower standard, with the Radicals demanding nearly impossible conditions for rebel states to return.

Lincoln's moderate plan for Reconstruction was actually part of his effort to win the war. Lincoln and the moderates felt that if it remained easy for states to return to the Union and if moderate proposals on black suffrage were made, that Confederate states involved in the hostilities might be swayed to re-join the Union rather than continue fighting. The radical plan was to ensure that reconstruction did not actually start until after the war was over.

In 1863 Abraham Lincoln was assassinated leaving Vice President Andrew Johnson to oversee the beginning of the actual implementation of Reconstruction. Johnson struck a moderate pose, willing to allow former confederates to keep control of their state governments. These governments quickly enacted Black Codes that denied the vote to blacks and granted them only limited civil rights.

The radical Republicans in Congress responded to the Black Codes by continuing their hard line on allowing former rebel states back into the Union. In addition, they sought to override the Black Codes by granting U.S. citizenship to blacks by passing a civil rights bill. Johnson, supported by Democrats, vetoed the bill, but Congress had the necessary votes to override it, and the bill became law.

In 1866, the Radical Republicans won control of Congress and passed the Reconstruction Acts, which placed the governments of the southern states under the control of the federal military. With this backing, the Republicans began to implement their radical policies such as granting all black men the vote and denying the vote to former confederate soldiers. Congress had passed the Thirteenth, Fourteenth, and Fifteenth Amendments granting citizenship and civil rights to blacks, and made ratification of these amendments a condition of readmission into the Union by the rebel states. The Republicans found support in the South among former slaves, white southerners who had not supported the Confederacy, called Scalawags, and northerners who had moved to the South and were known as Carpetbaggers.

Military control continued throughout Grant's administration, despite growing conflict both inside and outside the Republican Party. Conservatives in Congress and in the states opposed the liberal policies of the Republicans. Some Republicans became concerned over corruption issues among Grant's appointees and dropped support for him.

Under President Rutherford B. Hayes, the federal troops were removed from the South. Without this support, the Republican governments were replaced by so-called "redeemer governments," who promised the restoration of the vote to those whites who had been denied it and limitations on civil rights for blacks.

The rise of the redeemer governments marked the beginning of the Jim Crow laws and official segregation. Blacks were still allowed to vote, but ways were found to make it difficult for them to do so, such as literacy tests and poll taxes. Reconstruction, which had set as its goal the reunification of the South with the North and the granting of civil rights to freed slaves was a limited success, at best, and in the eyes of many blacks was considered a failure. However, before being allowed to rejoin the Union, the Confederate states were required to agree to all federal laws.

Skill 1.8   **Identify immigration and settlement patterns that have shaped the history of Florida.**

Florida's first human inhabitants were Indians, as shown by the burial mounds found in varying locations around the state. When Europeans eventually arrived, there were about 10,000 Indians belonging to as many as five major tribes. In the south, were the Calusa and the Tequesta; the Ais were found on the Atlantic coast in the central part of the peninsula; the Timucans were in the central and northeast area of the state; and in the northwest part of Florida dwelled the Apalachee.

Written records about life in Florida began with the arrival of the first European, Spanish explorer and adventurer Juan Ponce de León, in 1513, searching for the fabled fountain of youth. . Sometime between April 2 and April 8, Ponce de León waded ashore on the northeast coast of Florida, possibly near present-day St. Augustine. He called the area la Florida, in honor of Pascua Florida ("feast of the flowers"), Spain's Easter time celebration. Other Europeans may have reached Florida earlier, but no firm evidence of such achievement has been found.

The Spanish flag flew over Florida for the next 250 years. Other Spanish explorers who spent time in Florida included Panfilo de Narvaez, Hernando de Soto (who became the first European to reach the Mississippi River), and Pedro Menendez de Aviles (who put an end to French attempts to settle in eastern Florida and founded the first permanent European settlement in the present-day United States, St. Augustine).

On another voyage in 1521, Ponce de León landed on the southwestern coast of the peninsula, accompanied by two-hundred people, fifty horses, and numerous beasts of burden. His colonization attempt quickly failed because of attacks by native people. However, Ponce de León's activities served to identify Florida as a desirable place for explorers, missionaries, and treasure seekers.

In 1539, Hernando de Soto began another expedition in search of gold and silver on a long trek through Florida and what is now the southeastern United States. For four years, de Soto's expedition wandered, in hopes of finding the fabled wealth of the Indian people. De Soto and his soldiers camped for five months in the area now known as Tallahassee. De Soto died near the Mississippi River in 1542. Survivors of his expedition eventually reached Mexico.

No great treasure troves awaited the Spanish conquistadores who explored Florida. However, their stories helped inform Europeans about Florida and its relationship to Cuba, Mexico, and Central and South America, from which Spain regularly shipped gold, silver, and other products. Groups of heavily-laden Spanish vessels, called plate fleets, usually sailed up the Gulf Stream through the straits that parallel Florida's Keys. Aware of this route, pirates preyed on the fleets. Hurricanes created additional hazards, sometimes wrecking the ships on the reefs and shoals along Florida's eastern coast.

In 1559, Tristán de Luna y Arellano led another attempt by Europeans to colonize Florida. He established a settlement at Pensacola Bay, but a series of misfortunes caused his efforts to be abandoned after two years.

Spain was not the only European nation that found Florida attractive. In 1562, the French Protestant Jean Ribault explored the area. Two years later, fellow Frenchman René Goulaine de Laudonnière established Fort Caroline at the mouth of the St. Johns River, near present-day Jacksonville.

These French adventurers prompted Spain to accelerate her plans for colonization. Pedro Menéndez de Avilés hastened across the Atlantic, his sights set on removing the French and creating a Spanish settlement. Menéndez arrived in 1565 at a place he called San Augustín (St. Augustine) and established the first permanent European settlement in what is now the United States. He accomplished his goal of expelling the French, attacking and killing all settlers except for non-combatants and Frenchmen who professed belief in the Roman Catholic faith. Menéndez captured Fort Caroline and renamed it San Mateo.

French response came two years later, when Dominique de Gourgues recaptured San Mateo and made the Spanish soldiers stationed there pay with their lives. However, this incident did not halt the Spanish advance. Their pattern of constructing forts and Roman Catholic missions continued. Spanish missions established among native people soon extended across north Florida and as far north along the Atlantic coast as the area that we now call South Carolina.

The English, also eager to exploit the wealth of the Americas, increasingly came into conflict with Spain's expanding empire. In 1586 the English captain Sir Francis Drake looted and burned the tiny village of St. Augustine. However, Spanish control of Florida was not diminished.

In fact, as late as 1600, Spain's power over what is now the southeastern United States was unquestioned. When English settlers came to America, they established their first colonies well to the North—at Jamestown (in the present state of Virginia) in 1607 and Plymouth (in the present state of Massachusetts) in 1620. English colonists wanted to take advantage of the continent's natural resources and gradually pushed the borders of Spanish power southward into present-day southern Georgia. At the same time, French explorers were moving down the Mississippi River valley and eastward along the Gulf Coast.

The English colonists in the Carolina colonies were particularly hostile toward Spain. Led by Colonel James Moore, the Carolinians and their Creek Indian allies attacked Spanish Florida in 1702 and destroyed the town of St. Augustine. However, they could not capture the fort, named Castillo de San Marcos. Two years later, they destroyed the Spanish missions between Tallahassee and St. Augustine, killing many native people and enslaving many others. The French continued to harass Spanish Florida's western border and captured Pensacola in 1719, twenty-one years after the town had been established.

Spain's adversaries moved even closer when England founded Georgia in 1733, its southernmost continental colony. Georgians attacked Florida in 1740, assaulting the Castillo de San Marcos at St. Augustine for almost a month. While the attack was not successful, it did point out the growing weakness of Spanish Florida.

Britain gained control of Florida in 1763 in exchange for Havana, Cuba, which the British had captured from Spain during the Seven Years' War (1756–63). Spain evacuated Florida after the exchange, leaving the province virtually empty. At that time, St. Augustine was still a garrison community with fewer than five hundred houses, and Pensacola also was a small military town.

The British had ambitious plans for Florida. First, it was split into two parts: East Florida, with its capital at St. Augustine; and West Florida, with its seat at Pensacola. British surveyors mapped much of the landscape and coastline and tried to develop relations with a group of Indian people who were moving into the area from the North. The British called these people of Creek Indian descent **Seminolies, or Seminoles**. Britain attempted to attract white settlers by offering land on which to settle and help for those who produced products for export. Given enough time, this plan might have converted Florida into a flourishing colony, but British rule lasted only twenty years.

The two Florida's remained loyal to Great Britain throughout the War for American Independence (1776–83). However, Spain—participating indirectly in the war as an ally of France—captured Pensacola from the British in 1781. In 1784, it regained control of the rest of Florida as part of the peace treaty that ended the American Revolution. The second period of Spanish control lasted until 1821.

On one of those military operations, in 1818, General **Andrew Jackson** made a foray into Florida. Jackson's battles with Florida's Indian people later would be called the First Seminole War. When the British evacuated Florida, Spanish colonists as well as settlers from the newly formed United States came pouring in. Many of the new residents were lured by favorable Spanish terms for acquiring property, called land grants. Others who came were escaped slaves, trying to reach a place where their U.S. masters had no authority and effectively could not reach them. Instead of becoming more Spanish, the two Florida's increasingly became more "American." Finally, after several official and unofficial U.S. military expeditions into the territory, Spain formally ceded Florida to the United States in 1821, according to terms of the Adams-Onís Treaty.

Andrew Jackson returned to Florida in 1821 to establish a new territorial government on behalf of the United States. What the U.S. inherited was a wilderness sparsely dotted with settlements of native Indian people, African Americans, and Spaniards.

As a territory of the United States, Florida was particularly attractive to people from the older Southern plantation areas of Virginia, the Carolinas, and Georgia, who arrived in considerable numbers. After territorial status was granted, the two Florida's were merged into one entity with a new capital city in Tallahassee. Established in 1824, Tallahassee was chosen because it was halfway between the existing governmental centers of St. Augustine and Pensacola.

As Florida's population increased through immigration, so did pressure on the federal government to remove the Indian people from their lands. The Indian population was made up of several groups—primarily, the Creek and the Miccosukee people; and many African American refugees lived with the Indians. Indian removal was popular with white settlers because the native people occupied lands that white people wanted and because their communities often provided a sanctuary for runaway slaves from northern states.

Among Florida's native population, the name of Osceola has remained familiar after more than a century and a half. Osceola was a Seminole war leader who refused to leave his homeland in Florida. Seminoles, already noted for their fighting abilities, won the respect of U.S. soldiers for their bravery, fortitude, and ability to adapt to changing circumstances during the Second Seminole War (1835–42). This war, the most significant of the three conflicts between Indian people and U.S. troops in Florida, began over the question of whether Seminoles should be moved westward across the Mississippi River into what is now Oklahoma.

Under President Andrew Jackson, the U.S. government spent $20 million and the lives of many U.S. soldiers, Indian people, and U.S. citizens to force the removal of the Seminoles. In the end, the outcome was not as the federal government had planned. Some Indians migrated "voluntarily." Some were captured and sent west under military guard; and others escaped into the Everglades, where they made a life for themselves away from contact with whites.

Today, reservations occupied by Florida's Indian people exist at Immokalee, Hollywood, Brighton (near the city of Okeechobee), and along the Big Cypress Swamp. In addition to the Seminole people, Florida also has a separate Miccosukee tribe.

By 1840 white Floridians were concentrating on developing the territory and gaining statehood. The population had reached 54,477 people, with African American slaves making up almost one-half of the population. Steamboat navigation was well established on the Apalachicola and St. Johns Rivers, and railroads were planned.

Florida now was divided informally into three areas: East Florida, from the Atlantic Ocean to the Suwannee River; Middle Florida, between the Suwannee and the Apalachicola Rivers; and West Florida, from the Apalachicola to the Perdido River. The southern area of the territory (south of present-day Gainesville) was sparsely settled by whites. The territory's economy was based on agriculture. Plantations were concentrated in Middle Florida, and their owners established the political tone for all of Florida until after the Civil War.

Skill 1.9 **Identify significant individuals, events, and social, cultural, political, and economic characteristics of different periods throughout Florida's history.**

Florida became the twenty-seventh state in the United States on March 3, 1845. **William D. Moseley** was elected the new state's first governor, and David Levy Yulee, one of Florida's leading proponents for statehood, became a U.S. Senator. By 1850, the population had grown to 87,445, including about 39,000 African American slaves and 1,000 free blacks.

The slavery issue began to dominate the affairs of the new state. Most Florida voters—who were white males, ages twenty-one years or older—did not oppose slavery. However, they were concerned about the growing feeling against it in the North, and during the 1850s they viewed the new anti-slavery Republican party with suspicion. In the 1860 presidential election, no Floridians voted for Abraham Lincoln, although this Illinois Republican won at the national level. Shortly after his election, a special convention drew up an ordinance that allowed Florida to secede from the Union on January 10, 1861. Within several weeks, Florida joined other southern states to form the Confederate States of America.

During the Civil War, Florida was not ravaged as several other southern states were. Indeed, no decisive battles were fought on Florida soil. While Union forces occupied many coastal towns and forts, the interior of the state remained in Confederate hands.

Florida provided an estimated 15,000 troops and significant amounts of supplies—including salt, beef, pork, and cotton—to the Confederacy, but more than 2,000 Floridians, both African American and white, joined the Union army. Confederate and foreign merchant ships slipped through the Union navy blockade along the coast, bringing in needed supplies from overseas ports. Tallahassee was the only southern capital east of the Mississippi River to avoid capture during the war, spared by southern victories at Olustee (1864) and Natural Bridge (1865). Ultimately, the South was defeated, and federal troops occupied Tallahassee on May 10, 1865.

Before the Civil War, Florida had been well on its way to becoming another of the southern cotton states. Afterward, the lives of many residents changed. The ports of Jacksonville and Pensacola again flourished due to the demand for lumber and forest products to rebuild the nation's cities. Those who had been slaves were declared free. Plantation owners tried to regain prewar levels of production by hiring former slaves to raise and pick cotton. However, such programs did not work well, and much of the land came under cultivation by tenant farmers and sharecroppers, both African American and white.

Beginning in 1868, the federal government instituted a congressional program of "reconstruction" in Florida and the other southern states. During this period, Republican officeholders tried to enact sweeping changes, many of which were aimed at improving conditions for African Americans.

At the time of the 1876 presidential election, federal troops still occupied Florida. The state's Republican government and recently enfranchised African American voters helped to put Rutherford B. Hayes in the White House. However, Democrats gained control of enough state offices to end the years of Republican rule and prompt the removal of federal troops the following year. A series of political battles in the state left African Americans with little voice in their government.

During the final quarter of the nineteenth century, large-scale commercial agriculture in Florida, especially cattle-raising, grew in importance. Industries such as cigar manufacturing took root in the immigrant communities of the state. Large phosphate deposits were discovered, citrus groves were planted and cultivated, swamplands were drained, and **Henry Plant** and **Henry Flagler** built railroad lines opening the state for further growth and development.

Potential investors became interested in enterprises that extracted resources from the water and land. These extractive operations were as widely diverse as sponge harvesting in Tarpon Springs and phosphate mining in the southwestern part of the state. The Florida citrus industry grew rapidly, despite occasional freezes and economic setbacks. The development of industries throughout the state prompted the construction of roads and railroads on a large scale. Jobs created by the state helped develop the natural resources; private industries' construction of paper mills resulted in conservation programs for the state's forests and to help preserve perishable fruits and vegetables, cooling plants were built. To aid farmers, cooperative markets and cooperative farm groups were established.

Beginning in the 1870s, residents from northern states visited Florida as tourists to enjoy the state's natural beauty and mild climate. Steamboat tours on Florida's winding rivers were a popular attraction for these visitors.

The growth of Florida's transportation industry had its origins in 1855, when the state legislature passed the Internal Improvement Act. Like legislation passed by several other states and the federal government, Florida's act offered cheap or free public land to investors, particularly those interested in transportation. The act, and other legislation like it, had its greatest effect in the years between the end of the Civil War and the beginning of World War I. During this period, many railroads were constructed throughout the state by companies owned by Henry Flagler and Henry B. Plant, who also built lavish hotels near their railroad lines. The Internal Improvement Act stimulated the initial efforts to drain the southern portion of the state in order to convert it to farmland.

These development projects had far-reaching effects on the agricultural, manufacturing, and extractive industries of late nineteenth-century Florida. The citrus industry especially benefited, since it was now possible to pick oranges in south Florida; put them on a train heading north; and eat them in Baltimore, Philadelphia, or New York in less than a week.

In 1898, national attention focused on Florida, as the Spanish-American War began. The port city of Tampa served as the primary staging area for U.S. troops bound for the war in Cuba. Many Floridians supported the Cuban peoples' desire to be free of Spanish colonial rule.

By the turn of the century, Florida's population and per capita wealth were increasing rapidly; the potential of the "Sunshine State" appeared endless. By the end of World War I, land developers had descended on this virtual gold mine. With more Americans owning automobiles, it became commonplace to vacation in Florida. Many visitors stayed on, and exotic projects sprang up in southern Florida. Some people moved onto land made from drained swamps. Others bought canal-crossed tracts through what had been dry land. The real estate developments quickly attracted buyers, and land in Florida was sold and resold. Profits and prices for many developers reached inflated levels.

The early 1900s saw the settlement and economic development of south Florida, especially along the East Coast. A severe depression in 1926, the 1926 and 1928 hurricanes, and the Great Depression of the 1930s burst the economic bubble.

During World War II, many military bases were constructed as part of the vital defense interests of the state and nation. After the War, prosperity and population grew resulting in tourism becoming the most important industry and it remains so today. Continued agricultural development and industrial expansion also played an important role in the state's economy. Such industries as paper and paper products, chemicals, electronics, and ocean and space exploration gave a tremendous boost to the labor force. From the 1950s to the present day, The Kennedy Space Center at Cape Canaveral has been a space and rocket center with the launching of orbiting satellites, manned space flights and today's space shuttles.

There are serious problems to be faced. Many immigrants from places like Cuba and Haiti have entered the state by the thousands since the early 1960s, both legally and illegally. Increasing population growth puts a strain on public and social services and pollution and overbuilding has threatened the environment. Tremendous growth occurred during the 1970s with the opening of Walt Disney World. With other tourist attractions and the resulting need for hotels, restaurants, and a larger airport, Orlando leads Tampa, Miami, Jacksonville, Fort Lauderdale, and West Palm Beach as the fastest growing region of the state. Although the state's economy continues to rely mainly on tourism and the citrus industry, stable growth remains consistent due to the expanding trade, financial, and service industries.

COMPETENCY 2.0 KNOWLEDGE OF GEOGRAPHY

Skill 2.1 Identify essential themes and elements in geography and the terms associated with them.

GEOGRAPHY involves studying location and how living things and earth's features are distributed throughout the earth. It includes where animals, people, and plants live and the effects of their relationship with earth's physical features. Geographers also explore the locations of earth's features, how they got there, and why it is so important.

What geographers study can be broken down into five themes:

Location (including relative and absolute location) – A relative location refers to the surrounding geography, e.g., "on the banks of the Mississippi River." Absolute location refers to a specific point, such as 41 degrees North latitude, 90 degrees West longitude, or 123 Main Street.

Place - A place has both human and physical characteristics. Physical characteristics include features such as mountains, rivers, and deserts. Human characteristics are the features created by human interaction with the environment such as canals and roads.

Human-Environmental Interaction - The theme of human-environmental interaction has three main concepts: 1) humans adapt to the environment (wearing warm clothing in a cold climate, for instance); 2) humans modify the environment (planting trees to block a prevailing wind, for example); 3) and humans depend on the environment (for food, water and raw materials.

Movement - The theme of movement covers how humans interact with one another through trade, communications, emigration, and other forms of interaction.

Regions - A region is an area that has some kind of unifying characteristic, such as a common language or a common government. There are three main types of regions. 1) *Formal regions* are areas defined by actual political boundaries, such as a city, county, or state. 2) *Functional regions* are defined by a common function, such as the area covered by a telephone service. 2) *Vernacular regions* are less formally defined areas that are formed by people's perception, e.g., "the Middle East," or "the South."

Geographical studies are divided into:

Regional: Elements and characteristics of a place or region

Topical: One earth feature or one human activity occurring throughout the entire world

Physical: Earth's physical features, what creates and changes them, their relationships to each other as well as to human activities

Human: Human activity patterns and how they relate to the environment including political, cultural, historical, urban, and social geographical fields of study.

Special research methods used by geographers include mapping, interviewing, field studies, mathematics, statistics, and scientific instruments.

Skill 2.2   **Interpret maps and other geographic representations, tools, and technologies to acquire, process, and report information from a spatial perspective.**

We use **illustrations** of various sorts because it is often easier to demonstrate a given idea visually instead of orally. Sometimes it is even easier to do so with an illustration than a description. This is especially true in the areas of education and research because humans are visually stimulated. Any idea presented visually in some manner is always easier to understand and to comprehend than simply getting an idea across verbally, by hearing it or reading it. Throughout this document, there are several illustrations that have been presented to explain an idea in a more precise way. Sometimes these will demonstrate some of the types of illustrations available for use in the arena of political science. Among the more common illustrations used in geography and other disciplines are various types of **maps, graphs**, and **charts**.

Although maps have advantages over globes and photographs, they do have a major disadvantage: Most maps are flat and the Earth is a sphere. It is impossible to reproduce exactly on a flat surface a spherical object. In order to put the earth's features onto a map, the features must be stretched in some way. This stretching is called **distortion.** Distortion does not mean that maps are wrong. It simply means that they are not perfect representations of the Earth or its parts. **Cartographers,** or mapmakers, understand the problems of distortion. They try to design maps so that there is as little distortion as possible.

The process of putting the features of the Earth onto a flat surface is called **projection**. All maps are really map projections. Each of the different types deals in a different way with the problem of distortion. Map projections are made in a number of ways. Some are done using complicated mathematics. However, the basic ideas behind map projections can be understood by looking at the three most common types:

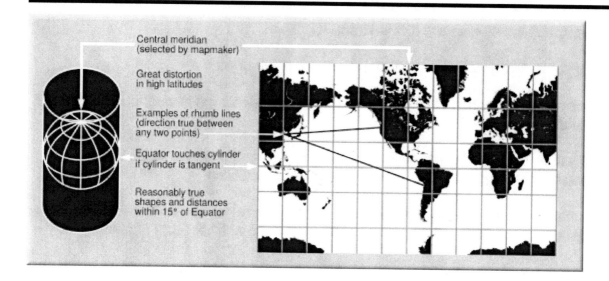

(1) **Cylindrical Projections** - These are done by taking a cylinder of paper and wrapping it around a globe. A light is used to project the globe's features onto the paper. Distortion is least where the paper touches the globe. For example, suppose that the paper was wrapped so that it touched the globe at the equator. The map from this projection would have just a little distortion near the equator. However, in moving north or south of the equator, the distortion would increase as you moved further away from the equator. The best known and most widely used cylindrical projection is the **Mercator Projection.** It was first developed in 1569 by Gerardus Mercator, a Flemish mapmaker.

(2). **Conical Projections** - The name for these maps comes from the projection being made onto a cone of paper. The cone is made so that it touches a globe at the base of the cone only. It can also be made so that it cuts through part of the globe in two different places. Again, there is the least distortion where the paper touches the globe. If the cone touches at two different points, there is some distortion at both of them. Conical projections are most often used to map areas in the **middle latitudes**. Maps of the United States are most often conical projections. This is because most of the country lies within these latitudes.

(3). **Flat-Plane** Projections - These are made with a flat piece of paper that touches the globe at one point only. Areas near this point show little distortion. Flat-plane projections are often used to show the areas of the north and south poles. One such flat projection is called a **Gnomonic Projection**. On this kind of map, all meridians appear as straight lines, Gnomonic projections are useful because any straight line drawn between points on it forms a **Great-Circle Route**.

Great-Circle Routes can best be described by thinking of a globe and how when using the globe, the shortest route between two points on it can be found by simply stretching a string from one point to the other. However, if the string was extended in reality so that it took into effect the globe's curvature, it would then make a great-circle. A great-circle is any circle that cuts a sphere, such as the globe, into two equal parts. Because of distortion, most maps do not show great-circle routes as straight lines, Gnomonic projections, however, do show the shortest distance between the two places as a straight line, and because of this, they are valuable for navigation. They are called Great-Circle Sailing Maps.

To properly analyze a given map one must be familiar with the various parts and symbols that most modern maps use. For the most part, this is standardized, with different maps using similar parts and symbols. These include:

The Title - All maps should have a title, just like all books should. The title tells you what information is to be found on the map.

The Legend - Most maps have a legend. A legend tells the reader about the various symbols that are used on that particular map and what the symbols represent (also called a *map key*).

The Grid - A grid is a series of lines that are used to find exact places and locations on the map. There are several different kinds of grid systems in use; however, most maps do use the longitude and latitude system, known as the

Geographic Grid System.

Directions - Most maps have some directional system to show which way the map is being presented. Often on a map, a small compass will be present, with arrows showing the four basic directions of north, south, east, and west.

The Scale - This is used to show the relationship between a unit of measurement on the map versus the real world measure on the Earth. Maps are drawn to many different scales. Some maps show a lot of detail for a small area. Others show a greater span of distance. One should always be aware of what scale is being used. For instance, the scale might be: 1 inch = 10 miles for a small area, or for a map showing the whole world, it might have a scale of 1 inch = 1,000 miles. The point is that one must look at the map key in order to see what units of measurements the map is using.

Maps have four main properties. They are 1) the size of the areas shown on the map; 2) the shapes of the areas; 3) consistent scales; and 4) straight line directions. A map can be drawn so that it is correct in one or more of these properties. No map can be correct in all of them.

Equal areas - One property that maps can have is that of equal areas, In an equal area map, the meridians and parallels are drawn so that the areas shown have the same proportions as they do on the Earth. For example, Greenland is about 118th the size of South America. Thus it will be show as 118th the size on an equal area map. The **Mercator projection** is an example of a map that does not have equal areas. In it, Greenland appears to be about the same size of South America. This is because the distortion becomes large at the poles, and Greenland lies near the North Pole.

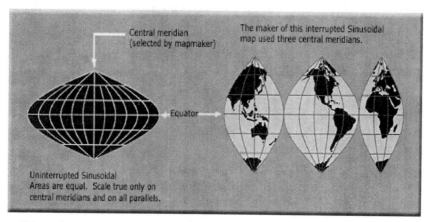

Conformality - A second map property is conformality, or correct shapes. There are no maps which can show very large areas of the earth in their exact shapes. Only globes can really do that, however Conformal Maps are as close as possible to true shapes. The United States is often shown by a Lambert Conformal Conic Projection Map.

Consistent Scales - Many maps attempt to use the same scale on all parts of the map. Generally, this is easier when maps show a relatively small part of the earth's surface. For example, a map of Florida might be a Consistent Scale Map. Generally maps showing large areas are not consistent-scale maps. This is so because of distortion. Often such maps will have two scales noted in the key. One scale, for example, might be accurate to measure distances between points along the Equator. Another might be then used to measure distances between the North Pole and the South Pole.

Maps showing physical features often try to show information about the elevation or *relief* of the land. *Elevation* is the distance above or below the sea level. The elevation is usually shown with colors. For instance, all areas on a map which are at a certain level will be shown in the same color.

Relief Maps - Show the shape of the land surface as flat, rugged, or steep. Relief maps usually give more detail than simply showing the overall elevation of the land's surface. Relief is also sometimes shown with colors, but another way to show relief is by using *contour lines*. These lines connect all points of a land surface which are the same height surrounding the particular area of land.

Thematic Maps - These are used to show more specific information, often on a single ***theme***, or topic. Thematic maps show the distribution or amount over a certain given area of things such as population density, climate, economic information, or cultural or political information.

Political science would be almost impossible without maps. Information can be gained looking at a map that might take hundreds of words to explain otherwise. Maps reflect the great variety of knowledge covered by political science. To show such a variety of information, maps are made in many different ways. Because of this variety, maps must be understood in order to make the best sense of them. Once they are understood, maps provide a solid foundation for political science studies.

To apply information obtained from ***graphs*** one must understand the two major reasons why graphs are used:

> 1. To present a <u>model or theory</u> visually in order to show how two or more variables interrelate.

> 2. To present <u>real world</u> data visually in order to show how two or more variables interrelate.

Most often used are those known as ***bar graphs*** and ***line graphs***. (Charts are often used for similar reasons and are explained in the next section.)

Graphs are most useful when one wishes to demonstrate the sequential increase, or decrease of a variable or to show specific correlations between two or more variables in a given circumstance.

Most common is the ***bar graph***, because it has a way of visually showing the difference in a given set of variables. However, it is limited in that it can not really show the actual proportional increase or decrease of each given variable to each other. (In order to show a decrease, a bar graph must show the "bar" under the starting line, thus removing the ability to really show how the various different variables would relate to each other.)

Thus in order to accomplish this one must use a **line graph**. Line graphs can be of two types a ***linear*** or ***non-linear*** graph. A linear line graph uses a series of straight lines a non-linear line graph uses a curved line. Though the lines can be either straight or curved, all of the lines are called ***curves***.

A line graph uses a number line or **axis.** The numbers are generally placed in order, equal distances from one another. The number line is used to represent a number, degree, or some such other variable at an appropriate point on the line. Two lines are used, intersecting at a specific point. They are referred to as the X-axis and the Y-axis. The Y-axis is a vertical line; the X-axis is a horizontal line. Together they form a **coordinate system.** The difference between a point on the line of the X-axis and the Y-axis is called the **slope** of the line, or the change in the value on the vertical axis divided by the change in the value on the horizontal axis. The Y-axis number is called the *rise* and the X-axis number is called the *run*, thus the equation for slope is:

SLOPE = RISE - *Change in value on the vertical axis*
RUN - *Change in value on the horizontal axis*

The slope tells the amount of increase or decrease of a given **specific** variable. When using two or more variables, one can plot the amount of difference between them in any given situation. This makes presenting information on a line graph more involved. It also makes it more informative and accurate than a simple bar graph. Knowledge of the term "slope" and understanding what it is and how it is measured helps us to describe verbally the pictures we are seeing visually. For example, if a curve is said to have a slope of "zero," you should picture a flat line. If a curve has a slope of "one," you should picture a rising line that makes a 45-degree angle with the horizontal and vertical axis lines.

The preceding examples are of **linear** (straight line) curves. With **non-linear** curves (the ones that really do curve), the slope of the curve is constantly changing, so as a result, we must then understand that the slope of the non-linear curved line will be at a specific point. How is this done? The slope of a non-linear curve is determined by the slope of a straight line *that intersects the curve at that specific point.*

In all graphs, an upward sloping line represents a direct relationship between the two variables. A downward slope represents an inverse relationship between the two variables. In reading any graph, one must always be very careful to understand what is being measured, what can be deduced, and what cannot be deduced from the given graph.

To use **charts** correctly, one should remember the reasons one uses graphs. The general ideas are similar. It is usually a question as to whether a graph or chart is more capable of adequately portraying the information one wants to illustrate. It is easy to see the difference between them and realize that in many ways graphs and charts are interrelated.

One of the most common types, because it is easiest to read and understand even for the layperson, is the **pie-chart.**

Pie-charts are used often, especially to illustrate the differences in percentages among various items or to demonstrate the divisions of a whole.

Realistically, a chart can be made out of almost any multiple set of variables. Remember to properly show the differences between them and what you are trying to prove and keep it clear enough to read and understand with a minimum of effort. The usefulness of a chart is wasted if too much time is taken in order to understand it. Charts are always used to *simplify* an idea, never to complicate it.

In geography and related fields, all type of illustrations, maps, graphs and charts are useful tools for both education and research. As such, they are quite often used to better demonstrate an idea rather than simply stating it because some problems and situations are easier to understand visually than verbally. The illustrations are also excellent for showing relationships between any given set of variables or circumstances. However, one must always remember that though a picture may "be worth a thousand words," it still can't say everything so one should always be aware of the limits of any diagrammatic model. In other words: "Seeing is not *always* believing."

Skill 2.3 Use mental maps to organize information about people, places, and environments.

Social science would be almost impossible to understand without maps. Actual physical maps often provide the foundation for the mental maps we use to understand social studies concepts. Information can be gained looking at a map that might take hundreds of words to explain otherwise. Maps reflect the great variety of knowledge covered by political science. To show such a variety of information maps are made in many different ways. Because of this variety, maps must be understood in order to make the best sense of them. Once they are understood, maps provide a solid foundation for social studies.

Two important terms in the study of geography that relate to mental maps are absolute and relative location. Both technically describe the same thing, but both are also, in many respects, as different as day and night.

First, what is **location**? We want to know this in order to determine where something is and where we can find it. We want to point to a spot on a map and say, "That is where we are" or "That is where we want to be." In another way, we want to know where something is as compared to other things. It is very difficult for many people to describe something without referring to something else. Associative reasoning is a powerful way to think.

Absolute location is the exact whereabouts of a person, place, or thing, according to any kind of geographical indicators you want to name. You could be talking about latitude and longitude or GPS or any kind of indicators at all. For example, Paris is at 48 degrees north longitude and 2 degrees east latitude. You can't get much more exact than that. If you had a map that showed every degree of latitude and longitude, you could pinpoint exactly where Paris was and have absolutely no doubt that your geographical depiction was accurate.

Many geographers prefer to use absolute location because of its precision. If you have access to maps and compasses and GPS indicators, why not describe the absolute location of something? It's much more accurate than other means of describing where something is. An absolute location can also be much simpler. Someone might ask you where the nearest post office is and you might say, "It's at the southeast corner of First Avenue and Main Street." That's about as absolute as you can get.

Relative location, on the other hand, is *always* a description that involves more than one thing. When you describe a relative location, you tell where something is by describing what is around it. The same description of where the nearest post office is in terms of absolute location might be this: "It's down the street from the supermarket, on the right side of the street, next to the dentist's office."

We use relative location to be not necessarily less precise but to be more in tune with the real world. Very few people carry exact maps or GPS locators around with them. Nearly everyone, though, can find a location if they have it described to them in terms of what is nearby.

Absolute location can be a bit more map-like and direction-oriented as well. You might say that Chicago is east of Seattle or that St. Louis is north of New Orleans. This is not nearly as involved as the post office location description. In the same way, you might say that Chicago is on Lake Michigan.

Spatial organization is a description of how things are grouped in a given space. In geographical terms, this can describe people, places, and environments anywhere and everywhere on Earth.

The most basic form of spatial organization for people is where they live. The vast majority of people live near other people, in villages and towns and cities and settlements. These people live near others in order to take advantage of the goods and services that naturally arise from cooperation. These villages and towns and cities and settlements are, to varying degrees, near bodies of water. Water is a staple of survival for every person on the planet and is also a good source of energy for factories and other industries, as well as a form of transportation for people and goods.

Skill 2.4   Analyze the factors (e.g., topographic, environmental, economic) that influence the selection of location for a specific activity (e.g., industrial and urban development, agriculture, transportation).

See Skills 2.7, 2.8, and 2.9

Skill 2.5   Interpret statistics that show how places differ in their human and physical characteristics.

See Skills 2.7, 2.8, and 2.9

Skill 2.6   Identify cultural, political, economic, sociological, and technological characteristics that define, link, or divide regions.

Physical **locations** of the earth's surface features include the four major hemispheres and the parts of the earth's continents in them. Political **locations** are the political divisions, if any, within each continent. Both physical and political locations are precisely determined in two *ways:* (1) Surveying is done to determine boundary lines and distance from other features. (2) Exact locations are precisely determined by imaginary lines of **latitude (parallels)** and **longitude (meridians)**. The intersection of these lines at right angles forms a grid, making it impossible to pinpoint an exact location of any place using any two grip coordinates.

The **Eastern Hemisphere,** located between the North and South Poles and between the Prime Meridian (0 degrees longitude) east to the International Date Line at 180 degrees longitude, consists of most of Europe, all of Australia, most of Africa, and all of Asia, except for a tiny piece of the easternmost part of Russia that extends east of 180 degrees longitude.

The **Western Hemisphere,** located between the North and South Poles and between the Prime Meridian (0 degrees longitude) west to the International Date Line at 180 degrees longitude, consists of all of North and South America, a tiny part of the easternmost part of Russia that extends east of 180 degrees longitude, and a part of Europe that extends west of the Prime Meridian (0 degrees longitude).

The **Northern Hemisphere,** located between the North Pole and the Equator, contains all of the continents of Europe and North America and parts of South America, Africa, and most of Asia.

The **Southern Hemisphere,** located between the South Pole and the Equator, contains all of Australia, a small part of Asia, about one-third of Africa, most of South America, and all of Antarctica.

Of the **seven continents,** only one contains just one entire country and is the only island continent, **Australia.** Its political divisions consist of six states and one territory: Western Australia, South Australia, Tasmania, Victoria, New South Wales, Queensland, and Northern Territory.

Africa is made up of 54 separate countries, the major ones being Egypt, Nigeria, South Africa, Zaire, Kenya, Algeria, Morocco, and the large island of Madagascar.

Asia consists of 49 separate countries, some of which include China, Japan, India, Turkey, Israel, Iraq, Iran, Indonesia, Jordan, Vietnam, Thailand, and the Philippines.

Europe's 43 separate nations include France, Russia, Malta, Denmark, Hungary, Greece, Bosnia, and Herzegovina.

North America consists of Canada, the United States of America, the island nations of the West Indies, and the "land bridge" of Middle America, including Cuba, Jamaica, Mexico, and Panama.

Thirteen separate nations together occupy the continent of **South America,** among them Brazil, Paraguay, Ecuador, and Suriname.

The continent of **Antarctica** has no political boundaries or divisions but has a number of science and research stations managed by nations such as Russia, Japan, France, Australia, and India.

The earth's surface is made up of 70% water and 30% land. Physical features of the land surface include mountains, hills, plateaus, valleys, and plains. Other minor landforms include deserts, deltas, canyons, mesas, basins, foothills, marshes and swamps. Earth's water features include oceans, seas, lakes, rivers, and canals.

Mountains are landforms with rather steep slopes at least 2,000 feet above sea level. Mountains are found in groups called mountain chains or mountain ranges. At least one range can be found on six of the earth's seven continents. North America has the Appalachian and Rocky Mountains; South America the Andes; Asia the Himalayas; Australia the Great Dividing Range; Europe the Alps; and Africa the Atlas, Ahaggar, and Drakensburg Mountains. Mountains are commonly formed by volcanic activity, or when land is thrust upward when two tectonic plates collide.

Hills are elevated landforms rising to an elevation of about 500 to 2000 feet. They are found everywhere on earth including Antarctica where they are covered by ice.

Plateaus are elevated landforms usually level on top. Depending on location, they range from being an area that is very cold to one that is cool and healthful. Some plateaus are dry because they are surrounded by mountains that keep out any moisture. An example is the Kenya Plateau in East Africa, which is very cool. The plateau extending north from the Himalayas is extremely dry while those in Antarctica and Greenland are covered with ice and snow. Plateaus can be formed by underground volcanic activity, erosion, or colliding tectonic plates.

Plains are described as areas of flat or slightly rolling land, usually lower than the landforms next to them. Sometimes called lowlands (and sometimes located along **seacoasts)**, they support the majority of the world's people. Some are found inland, and many have been formed by large rivers. This results in extremely fertile soil for successful cultivation of crops and results in numerous and large settlements of people. In North America, the vast plains extend from the Gulf of Mexico north to the Arctic Ocean and between the Appalachian and Rocky Mountains. In Europe, rich plains extend east from Great Britain into central Europe and on into the Siberian region of Russia. Plains in river valleys are found in China (the Yangtze River valley), India (the Ganges River valley), and Southeast Asia (the Mekong River valley).

Valleys are land areas that are found between hills and mountains. Some have gentle slopes containing trees and plants; others have very steep walls and are referred to as canyons. One famous example is Arizona's Grand Canyon of the Colorado River, which was formed by erosion.

Deserts are large dry areas of land receiving ten inches or less of rainfall each year. Among the better known deserts are Africa's large Sahara Desert, the Arabian Desert on the Arabian Peninsula, and the desert Outback covering roughly one third of Australia. Deserts are found mainly in the tropical latitudes, and are formed when surrounding features such as mountain ranges extract most of the moisture from the prevailing winds

Deltas are areas of lowlands formed by soil and sediment deposited at the mouths of rivers. The soil is generally very fertile, and most fertile river deltas are important crop-growing areas. One well-known example is the delta of Egypt's Nile River, known for its production of cotton.

Mesas are the flat tops of hills or mountains usually with steep sides. Mesas are similar to plateaus, but smaller.

Basins are considered to be low areas drained by rivers or low spots in mountains.

Foothills are generally considered a low series of hills found between a plain and a mountain range.

Marshes and swamps are wet lowlands providing growth of such plants as rushes and reeds.

Oceans are the largest bodies of water on the planet. The four oceans of the earth are the **Atlantic Ocean**, one-half the size of the Pacific and separating North and South America from Africa and Europe; the **Pacific Ocean**, covering almost one-third of the entire surface of the earth and separating North and South America from Asia and Australia; the **Indian Ocean**, touching Africa, Asia, and Australia; and the ice-filled **Arctic Ocean,** extending from North America and Europe to the North Pole. The waters of the Atlantic, Pacific, and Indian Oceans also touch the shores of Antarctica.

Seas are smaller than the Atlantic or Pacific oceans and are partially surrounded by land. Some examples include the Mediterranean Sea found between Europe, Asia, and Africa; and the Caribbean Sea, touching the West Indies, South and Central America.

A **lake** is a body of standing water surrounded by land. The Great Lakes in North America are a good example. The deepest lake in the world is Lake Baikal in Siberia which contains as much water as all the Great Lakes put together.

Rivers, considered a nation's lifeblood, begin as very small streams, formed by melting snow and rainfall, flowing from higher to lower land, emptying into a larger body of water, usually a sea or an ocean. Examples of important rivers for the people and countries affected by and/or dependent on them include the Nile, Niger, and Zaire Rivers of Africa; the Rhine, Danube, and Thames Rivers of Europe; the Yangtze, Ganges, Mekong, Hwang He, and Irrawaddy Rivers of Asia; the Murray-Darling in Australia; and the Orinoco in South America. River systems are made up of large rivers and numerous smaller rivers or tributaries flowing into them. Examples include the vast Amazon Rivers system in South America and the Mississippi River system in the United States.

Canals are man-made water passages constructed to connect two larger bodies of water. Famous examples include the **Panama Canal** across Panama's isthmus connecting the Atlantic and Pacific Oceans and the **Suez Canal** in the Middle East between Africa and the Arabian peninsulas connecting the Red and Mediterranean Seas.

Social scientists use the term **culture** to describe the way of life of a group of people. This would include not only art, music, and literature but also beliefs, customs, languages, traditions, inventions—in short, any way of life whether complex or simple. The term geography is defined as the study of earth's features and living things as to their location, relationship with each other, how they came to be there, and why so important.

Physical geography is concerned with the locations of such earth features as climate, water, and land and how these relate to and affect each other and human activities; and what forces shaped and changed them. All three of these earth features affect the lives of all humans having a direct influence on what is made and produced, where it occurs, how it occurs, and what makes it possible. The combination of the different climate conditions and types of landforms and other surface features work together all around the earth to give the many varied cultures their unique characteristics and distinctions.

Cultural geography studies the location, characteristics, and influence of the physical environment on different cultures around the earth. Also included in these studies are comparisons and influences of the many varied cultures. Ease of travel and up-to-the-minute, state-of-the-art communication techniques ease the difficulties of understanding cultural differences making it easier to come in contact with them.

Skill 2.7   Identify ways in which people adapt to an environment through the production and use of clothing, food, and shelter.

Human communities subsisted initially as gatherers – gathering berries, leaves, etc. With the invention of tools it became possible to dig for roots, hunt small animals, and catch fish from rivers and oceans. Humans observed their environments and soon learned to plant seeds and harvest crops. As people migrated to areas in which game and fertile soil were abundant, communities began to develop. When people had the knowledge to grow crops and the skills to hunt game, they began to understand division of labor. Some of the people in the community tended to agricultural needs while others hunted game.

As habitats attracted larger numbers of people, environments became crowded and there was competition. The concept of division of labor and sharing of food soon came, in more heavily populated areas, to be managed. Groups of people focused on growing crops while others concentrated on hunting. Experience led to the development of skills and of knowledge that make the work easier. Farmers began to develop new plant species and hunters began to protect animal species from other predators for their own use. This ability to manage the environment led people to settle down, to guard their resources, and to manage them.

Camps soon became villages. Villages became year-round settlements. Animals were domesticated and gathered into herds that met the needs of the village. With the settled life it was no longer necessary to "travel light." Pottery was developed for storing and cooking food.

By 8000 BCE, culture was beginning to evolve in these villages. Agriculture was developed for the production of grain crops, which led to a decreased reliance on wild plants. Domesticating animals for various purposes decreased the need to hunt wild game. Life became more settled. It was then possible to turn attention to such matters as managing water supplies, producing tools, making cloth, etc.

There was both the social interaction and the opportunity to reflect upon existence. Mythologies arose and various kinds of belief systems. Rituals arose that re-enacted the mythologies that gave meaning to life.

As farming and animal husbandry skills increased, the dependence upon wild game and food gathering declined. With this change came the realization that a larger number of people could be supported on the produce of farming and animal husbandry.

Two things seem to have come together to produce cultures and civilizations: a society and culture based on agriculture and the development of centers of the community with literate social and religious structures. The members of these hierarchies then managed water supply and irrigation, ritual and religious life, and exerted their own right to use a portion of the goods produced by the community for their own subsistence in return for their management.

Sharpened skills, development of more sophisticated tools, commerce with other communities, and increasing knowledge of their environment, the resources available to them, and responses to the needs to share goods, order community life, and protect their possessions from outsiders led to further division of labor and community development.

As trade routes developed and travel between cities became easier, trade led to specialization. Trade enables a people to obtain the goods they desire in exchange for the goods they are able to produce. This, in turn, leads to increased attention to refinements of technique and the sharing of ideas. The knowledge of a new discovery or invention provides knowledge and technology that increases the ability to produce goods for trade.

As each community learns the value of the goods it produces and improves its ability to produce the goods in greater quantity, industry is born.

Skill 2.8 Evaluate the effects of human activity and technology on the environment.

Humans have always turned to nature for resources, from wood for the first cooking fires, to iron ore for the first metal tools, to crude oil to refine into fuel for automobiles and airplanes. Some of these resources, such as oil and metal ores, have a large, but limited supply. This kind of resource is considered non-renewable; once it has all been used, more cannot be made.

Natural resources that are virtually unlimited in supply, or which can be grown, are considered renewable resources. Trees that supply wood for construction and paper are considered renewable resources if managed correctly. Solar and wind energy are renewable resources because their supply is practically infinite. Hydrogen is a potential renewable resource that is receiving increasing attention because it can be derived from water, which is virtually unlimited.

Since the dawn of agriculture, humans have modified their environment to suit their needs and to provide food and shelter. Agriculture, for instance, often involves loosening topsoil by plowing before planting. This in turn affects how water and wind act on the soil and can lead to erosion. In extreme cases, erosion can leave a plot of agricultural land unsuitable for use. Modern methods of farming rely less on plowing the soil before planting, but more on chemical fertilizers, pesticides, and herbicides. However, these chemicals can find their way into groundwater, affecting the environment.

Cities show how humans modify their environment to suit their needs. Cities have a major impact on the environment. Concentrated consumption of fuels by automobiles and home heating systems affect the quality of the air in and around cities. The lack of exposed ground means that rainwater runs off roads and rooftops into sewer systems instead of seeping into the ground, often making its way into nearby streams or rivers and carrying urban debris with it.

Most countries recognize the importance of limiting the impact human populations have on the environment and have laws in place toward this goal. Emissions of certain compounds by factories, power plants, automobiles, and other sources are regulated. Cities collect sewage water into plants where it is treated before returning to rivers and streams. Incentives have been put in place in some areas to encourage people to use cleaner, alternative fuel sources, and many governments are supporting research into new sources of fuel that will reduce the reliance on non-renewable resources.

Ecology is the study of how living organisms interact with the physical aspects of their surroundings (their environment) including soil, water, air, and other living things.

Biogeography is the study of how the surface features of the earth – form, movement, and climate–affect living things.

Three levels of environmental understanding are critical. An **ecosystem** is a community consisting of a physical environment and the organisms that live within it. A **biome** is a large area of land with characteristic climate, soil, and a mixture of plants and animals. Biomes are made up of groups of ecosystems. Major biomes include deserts, chaparrals, savannas, tropical rain forests, temperate grasslands, temperate deciduous forests, taigas, and tundras. A **habitat** is the set of surroundings within which members of a species normally live. Elements of the habitat include soil, water, predators, and competitors.

Within habitats interactions between members of the species occur. These interactions occur between members of the same species and between members of different species. Interaction tends to be of three types: competition, predation, or symbiosis.

Competition occurs between members of the same species or between members of different species for resources required to continue life, to grow, or to reproduce. For example, competition for acorns can occur between squirrels or it can occur between squirrels and woodpeckers. One species can either push out or cause the demise of another species if it is better adapted to obtain the resource. When a new species is introduced into a habitat, the result can be a loss of the native species and/or significant change to the habitat. For example, the introduction of the Asian plant Kudzu into the American South has resulted in the destruction of several species because Kudzu grows and spreads very quickly and smothers everything in its path.

Predation occurs when organisms live by hunting and eating other organisms. The species best suited for hunting other species in the habitat will be the species that survives. Larger, predator species with better hunting skills reduce the amount of prey available for smaller and/or weaker species. This affects both the amount of available prey and the diversity of species that are able to survive in the habitat.

Symbiosis is a condition in which two organisms of different species are able to live in the same environment over an extended period of time without harming one another. In some cases, one species may benefit without harming the other. In other cases, both species benefit.

By nature, different organisms are best suited for existence in particular environments. When an organism is displaced to a different environment or when the environment changes for some reason, its ability to survive is determined by its ability to **adapt** to the new environment. Adaptation can take the form of structural change, physiological change, or behavioral modification.

Biodiversity refers to the variety of species and organisms, as well as the variety of habitats, available on the earth. Biodiversity provides the life-support system for the various habitats and species. The greater the degree of biodiversity, the more species and habitats will continue to survive.

Natural changes occur that can alter habitats (floods, volcanoes, storms, earthquakes). These changes can affect the species that exist within the habitat either by causing extinction or by changing the environment in a way that will no longer support the life systems. Climate changes can have similar effects. Inhabiting species, however, can also alter habitats particularly through migration. Human civilization, population growth, and efforts to control the environment can have many negative effects on various habitats. Humans change their environments to suit their particular needs and interests.

This can result in changes that result in the extinction of species or changes to the habitat itself. For example, deforestation damages the stability of mountain surfaces. One particularly devastating example is in the removal of the grasses of the Great Plains for agriculture. Tilling the ground and planting crops left the soil unprotected. Sustained drought dried the soil into dust. When wind storms occurred, the topsoil was stripped away and blown all the way to the Atlantic Ocean.

The interrelationship of environmental and social policy

The purpose and aim of social policy is to **improve human welfare** and to **meet basic human** needs within the society. **Social policy** addresses basic human needs for the sustainability of the individual and the society. The concerns of social policy, then, include food, clean water, shelter, clothing, education, health, and social security. Social policy is part of **public policy**, determined by the city, the state, the nation, or the multi-national organization responsible for human welfare in a particular region.

Environmental policy is concerned with the sustainability of the earth, the region under the administration of the governing group or individual or a local habitat. The concern of environmental policy is the preservation of the region, habitat or ecosystem.

Because humans, both individually and in community, rely upon the environment to sustain human life, social and environmental policy must be mutually supportable. Because humans, both individually and in community, live upon the earth, draw upon the natural resources of the earth, and affect the environment in many ways, environmental and social policy must be mutually supportive.

If modern societies have no understanding of the limitations upon natural resources or how their actions affect the environment, and they act without regard for the sustainability of the earth, it will become impossible for the earth to sustain human existence. At the same time, the resources of the earth are necessary to support the human welfare. Environmental policies must recognize that the planet is the home of humans and other species.

For centuries, social policies, economic policies, and political policies have ignored the impact of human existence and human civilization upon the environment. Human civilization has disrupted the ecological balance, contributed to the extinction of animal and plant species, and destroyed ecosystems through uncontrolled harvesting.

In an age of global warming, unprecedented demand upon natural resources, and a shrinking planet, social and environmental policies must become increasingly interdependent if the planet is to continue to support life and human civilization.

Skill 2.9 **Identify physical, cultural, social, economic, and political reasons for the movement of people in the world, nation, or state.**

By nature, people are essentially social creatures. They generally live in communities or settlements of some kind and of some size. Settlements are the cradles of culture, political structure, education, and the management of resources. The relative placement of these settlements or communities are shaped by the proximity to natural resources, the movement of raw materials, the production of finished products, the availability of a work force, and the delivery of finished products. The composition of communities will, at least to some extent, be determined by shared values, language, culture, religion, and subsistence.

Settlements begin in areas that offer the natural resources to support life – food and water. With the ability to manage the environment one finds a concentration of populations. With the ability to transport raw materials and finished products, comes mobility. With increasing technology and the rise of industrial centers, comes a migration of the workforce.

Cities are the major hubs of human settlement. Almost half of the population of the world now lives in cities. These percentages are much higher in developed regions. Established cities continue to grow. The fastest growth, however, is occurring in developing areas. In some regions there are "**metropolitan areas**" made up of urban and sub-urban areas. In some places cities and urban areas have become interconnected into "**megalopoli**" (e.g., Tokyo-Kawasaki-Yokohama).

The concentrations of populations and the divisions of these areas among various groups that constitute the cities can differ significantly. North American cities are different from European cities in terms of shape, size, population density, and modes of transportation. While in North America, the wealthiest economic groups tend to live outside the cities, the opposite is true in Latin American cities.

There are significant differences among the cities of the world in terms of connectedness to other cities. While European and North American cities tend to be well linked both by transportation and communication connections, there are other places in the world in which communication between the cities of the country may be inferior to communication with the rest of the world.

Rural areas tend to be less densely populated due to the needs of agriculture. More land is needed to produce crops or for animal husbandry than for manufacturing, especially in a city in which the buildings tend to be taller. Rural areas, however, must be connected via communication and transportation in order to provide food and raw materials to urban areas.

Skill 2.10 **Analyze factors contributing to the level of economic development in various geographic regions.**

The **Agricultural Revolution**, initiated by the invention of the plow, led to a thoroughgoing transformation of human society by making large-scale agricultural production possible and facilitating the development of agrarian societies. During the period during which the plow was invented, the wheel, numbers, and writing were also invented. Coinciding with the shift from hunting wild game to the domestication of animals, this period was one of dramatic social and economic change.

Numerous changes in lifestyle and thinking accompanied the development of stable agricultural communities. Rather than gathering a wide variety of plants as hunter-gatherers, agricultural communities become dependent on a limited number of plants or crops that are harvested. Subsistence becomes vulnerable to the weather and dependent upon planting and harvesting times.

Agriculture also required a great deal of physical labor and the development of a sense of discipline. Agricultural communities become sedentary or stable in terms of location. This makes the construction of dwellings appropriate. These tend to be built relatively close together, creating villages or towns.

Stable communities also free people from the need to carry everything with them and the move from hunting ground to hunting ground. This facilitates the invention of larger, more complex tools. As new tools are envisioned and developed it begins to make sense to have some specialization within the society. Skills begin to have greater value, and people begin to do work on behalf of the community that utilizes their particular skills and abilities. Settled community life also gives rise to the notion of wealth. It is now possible to keep possessions.

In the beginning of the transition to agriculture, the tools that were used for hunting and gathering were adequate to the tasks of agriculture. The initial challenge was in adapting to a new way of life. Once that challenge was met, attention turned to the development of more advanced tools and sources of energy. Six thousand years ago the first plow was invented in Mesopotamia. This plow was pulled by animals. Agriculture was now possible on a much larger scale. Soon tools were developed that make such basic tasks as gathering seeds, planting, and cutting grain faster and easier.

It also becomes necessary to maintain social and political stability to ensure that planting and harvesting times are not interrupted by internal discord or a war with a neighboring community. It also becomes necessary to develop ways to store the crop and prevent its destruction by the elements and animals. And then it must be protected from thieves.

Settled communities that produce the necessities of life are self-supporting. Advances in agricultural technology and the ability to produce a surplus of produce create two opportunities: first, the opportunity to trade the surplus goods for other desired goods, and second, the vulnerability to others who steal to take those goods. Protecting domesticated livestock and surplus, as well as stored, crops become an issue for the community. This, in turn, leads to the construction of walls and other fortifications around the community.

The ability to produce surplus crops creates the opportunity to trade or barter with other communities in exchange for desired goods. Traders and trade routes begin to develop between villages and cities. The domestication of animals expands the range of trade and facilitates an exchange of ideas and knowledge.

The **Industrial Revolution** of the eighteenth and nineteenth centuries resulted in even greater changes in human civilization and even greater opportunities for trade, increased production, and the exchange of ideas and knowledge.

The first phase of the Industrial Revolution (1750-1830) saw the mechanization of the textile industry, vast improvements in mining, with the invention of the steam engine, and numerous improvements in transportation, with the development and improvement of turnpikes, canals, and the invention of the railroad.

The second phase (1830-1910) resulted in vast improvements in a number of industries that had already been mechanized through such inventions as the Bessemer steel process and the invention of steam ships. New industries arose as a result of the new technological advances, such as photography, electricity, and chemical processes. New sources of power were harnessed and applied, including petroleum and hydroelectric power. Precision instruments were developed and engineering was launched. It was during this second phase that the Industrial Revolution spread to other European countries, to Japan, and to the United States.

The direct results of the industrial revolution, particularly as they affected industry, commerce, and agriculture, included:

- Enormous increases in productivity
- Huge increases in world trade
- Specialization and division of labor
- Standardization of parts and mass production
- Growth of giant business conglomerates and monopolies
- A new revolution in agriculture facilitated by the steam engine, machinery, chemical fertilizers, processing, canning, and refrigeration

The political results included:

- Growth of complex government by technical experts
- Centralization of government, including regulatory administrative agencies
- Advantages to democratic development, including extension of franchise to the middle class, and later to all elements of the population, mass education to meet the needs of an industrial society, the development of media of public communication, including radio, television, and cheap newspapers
- Dangers to democracy included the risk of manipulation of the media of mass communication, facilitation of dictatorial centralization and totalitarian control, subordination of the legislative function to administrative directives, efforts to achieve uniformity and conformity, and social impersonalization.

The economic results were numerous:

- The conflict between free trade and low tariffs and protectionism
- The issue of free enterprise against government regulation
- Struggles between labor and capital, including the trade-union movement
- The rise of socialism
- The rise of the utopian socialists
- The rise of Marxian or scientific socialism

The social results of the Industrial Revolution include:

- Increase of population, especially in industrial centers
- Advances in science applied to agriculture, sanitation and medicine
- Growth of great cities
- Disappearance of the difference between city dwellers and farmers
- Faster tempo of life and increased stress from the monotony of the work routine
- The emancipation of women
- The decline of religion
- Rise of scientific materialism
- Darwin's theory of evolution

Increased mobility produced a rapid diffusion of knowledge and ideas. Increased mobility also resulted in wide-scale immigration to industrialized countries. Cultures clashed and cultures melded.

Skill 2.11   Identify several examples of interdependence between regions of the world.

Competition for control of areas of the earth's surface is a common trait of human interaction throughout history. This competition has resulted in both destructive conflict and peaceful and productive cooperation. Societies and groups have sought control of regions of the earth's surface for a wide variety of reasons including religion, economics, politics and administration. Numerous wars have been fought through the centuries for the control of territory for each of these reasons.

At the same time, groups of people, even societies, have peacefully worked together to establish boundaries around regions or territories that served specific purposes in order to sustain the activities that support life and social organization.

Individuals and societies have divided the earth's surface through conflict for a number of reasons:

- The domination of peoples or societies, e.g., colonialism
- The control of valuable resources, e.g., oil
- The control of strategic routes, e.g., the Panama Canal

Conflicts can be spurred by religion, political ideology, national origin, language, and race. Conflicts can result from disagreement over how land, ocean or natural resources will be developed, shared, and used. Conflicts have resulted from trade, migration, and settlement rights. Conflicts can occur between small groups of people, between cities, between nations, between religious groups, and between multi-national alliances.

Today, the world is primarily divided by political/administrative interests into state sovereignties. A particular region is recognized to be controlled by a particular government, including its territory, population and natural resources. The only area of the earth's surface that today is not defined by state or national sovereignty is Antarctica.

Alliances are developed among nations on the basis of political philosophy, economic concerns, cultural similarities, religious interests, or for military defense.

Some of the most notable alliances today are:
- The United Nations
- The North Atlantic Treaty Organization
- The Caribbean Community
- The Common Market
- The Council of Arab Economic Unity
- The European Union

Large companies and multi-national corporations also compete for control of natural resources for manufacturing, development, and distribution.

Throughout human history there have been conflicts on virtually every scale over the right to divide the Earth according to differing perceptions, needs and values. These conflicts have ranged from tribal conflicts to urban riots, to civil wars, to regional wars, to world wars. While these conflicts have traditionally centered on control of land surfaces, new disputes are beginning to arise over the resources of the oceans and space.

On smaller scales, conflicts have created divisions between rival gangs, use zones in cities, water supply, school districts; economic divisions include franchise areas and trade zones.

COMPETENCY 3.0 KNOWLEDGE OF CIVICS AND GOVERNMENT

Skill 3.1 Identify the structure, functions, and purposes of government.

Purpose and function of government

Historically the functions of government, or people's concepts of government and its purpose and function, have varied considerably. In the theory of political science, the function of government is to secure the common welfare of the members of the given society over which it exercises control. In different historical eras, governments have attempted to achieve the common welfare by various means in accordance with the traditions and ideology of the given society.

Among primitive peoples, systems of control were rudimentary at best. They arose directly from the ideas of right and wrong that had been established in the group and were common in that particular society. Control being exercised most often by means of group pressure, most often in the forms of taboos and superstitions and in many cases by ostracism, or banishment from the group. Thus, in most cases, because of the extreme tribal nature of society in those early times, this led to very unpleasant circumstances for the individual so treated. Without the protection of the group, a lone individual was most often in for a sad and very short, fate. (No other group would accept such an individual into their midst and survival alone was extremely difficult if not impossible).

Among more civilized peoples, governments began to assume more institutional forms. They rested on a well-defined legal basis. They imposed penalties on violators of the social order. They used force, which was supported and sanctioned by their people. The government was charged to establish the social order and was supposed to do so in order to be able to discharge its functions.

Eventually the ideas of government, who should govern and how, came to be considered by various thinkers and philosophers. The most influential of these and those who had the most influence on our present society were the ancient Greek philosophers such as Plato and Aristotle.

Aristotle's conception of government was based on a simple idea. The function of government was to provide for the general welfare of its people. A good government, and one that should be supported, was one that did so in the best way possible, with the least pressure on the people. Bad governments were those that subordinated the general welfare to that of the individuals who ruled. At no time should any function of any government be that of personal interest of any one individual, no matter who that individual was. This does not mean that Aristotle had no sympathy for the individual or individual happiness (as at times Plato has been accused by those who read his "**Republic,**" which was the first important philosophical text to explore these issues). Rather Aristotle believed that a society is greater than the sum of its parts, or that "the good of the many outweighs the good of the few and also of the one".

Government began as a form of protection. A strong person, usually one of the best warriors or someone who had the support of many strong men, assumed command of a people or a city or a land. The power to rule those people rested in his hands. (The vast majority of rulers throughout history have been male.) Laws existed insofar as the pronouncements and decision of the ruler and were not, in practice, written down, leading to inconsistency. Religious leaders had a strong hand in governing the lives of people, and in many instances the political leader was also the primary religious figure.

First in Greece and then in Rome and then in other places throughout the world, the idea of government by more than one person or more than just a handful came to the fore. Even though more people were involved, the purpose of government hadn't changed. These governments still existed to keep the peace and protect their people from encroachments by both inside and outside forces.

Through the Middle Ages and on into even the 20th century, many countries still had **monarchs** as their heads of state. These monarchs made laws (or, later, upheld laws), but the laws were still designed to protect the welfare of the people—and the state.

In the modern day, people are subject to **laws** made by many levels of government. Local governments such as city and county bodies are allowed to pass ordinances covering certain local matters, such as property taxation, school districting, civil infractions and business licensing. These local bodies have perhaps the least political power in the governmental hierarchy, but being small and relatively accessible, they are often the level at which many citizens become directly involved with government. Funding for local governments often comes from property and sales taxes.

Federal, state, local, and tribal governments in the United States

The various governments of the United States and of Native American tribes have many similarities and a few notable differences. They are more similar than not; and all in all, they reflect the tendency of their people to prefer a representative that has checks and balances that look after one another and the people that keep them in power.

The national or federal government of the United States derives its power from the US Constitution and has three branches, the legislative, executive and judicial. The federal government exists to make national policy and to legislate matters that affect the residents of all states, and to settle matters between states. National income tax is the primary source for federal funding.

The US Constitution also provides the federal government with the authority to make treaties and enter agreements with foreign countries, creating a body of international law. While there is no authoritative international government, organizations such as the United Nations, the European Union and other smaller groups exist to promote economic and political cooperation between nations.

The **United States government** has three distinct branches: the Executive, the Legislative, and the Judicial. Each has its own function and its own "check" on the other two.

The Legislative Branch consists primarily of the House of Representatives and the Senate. Each house has a set number of members, the House having 435 apportioned according to national population trends and the Senate having 100 (two for each state). House members serve two-year terms; Senators serve six-year terms. Each house can initiate a bill, but that bill must be passed by a majority of both houses in order to become a law. The House is primarily responsible for initiating spending bills; the Senate is responsible for ratifying treaties that the President might sign with other countries.

The Executive Branch has the President and Vice-President as its two main figures. The President is the commander-in-chief of the armed forces and the person who can approve or veto all bills from Congress. (Vetoed bills can become law anyway if two-thirds of each house of Congress vote to pass it over the President's objections.) The President is elected to a four-year term by the Electoral College, which usually mirrors the popular will of the people. The President can serve a total of two terms. The Executive Branch also has several departments consisting of advisors to the President. These departments include State, Defense, Education, Treasury, and Commerce, among others. Members of these departments are appointed by the President and approved by Congress.

The Judicial Branch consists of a series of courts and related entities, with the top body being the Supreme Court. The Court decides whether laws of the land are constitutional; any law invalidated by the Supreme Court is no longer in effect. The Court also regulates the enforcement and constitutionality of the Amendments to the Constitution. The Supreme Court is the highest court in the land. Cases make their way to it from federal Appeals Courts, which hear appeals of decisions made by federal District Courts. These lower two levels of courts are found in regions around the country. Supreme Court Justices are appointed by the President and confirmed by the Senate. They serve for life. Lower-court judges are elected in popular votes within their states.

State governments are mainly patterned after the federal government, with an elected legislative body, a judicial system, and a governor who oversees the executive branch, with one important exception: governors are not technically commanders in chief of armed forces;. Like the federal government, state governments derive their authority from **constitutions**. State legislation applies to all residents of that state, and local laws must conform. State government funding is frequently from state income tax and sales taxes. State supreme court decisions can be appealed to federal courts and judges, even of the state supreme courts, are elected by popular vote. State representatives, senators, and governors have term limits that vary by state.

Local governments vary widely across the country, although none of them has a judicial branch per se. Some local governments consist of a city council, of which the mayor is a member and has limited powers; in other cities, the mayor is the head of the government and the city council are the chief lawmakers. Local governments also have less strict requirements for people running for office than do the state and federal governments.

The format of the governments of the various Native American tribes varies as well. Most tribes have governments along the lines of the U.S. federal or state governments. An example is the Cherokee Nation, which has a 15-member **Tribal Council** as the head of the Legislative branch, a Principal Chief and Deputy Chief who head up the Executive branch and carry out the laws passed by the Tribal Council, and a Judicial branch made up of the Judicial Appeals Tribunal and the Cherokee Nation District Court. Members of the Tribunal are appointed by the Principal Chief. Members of the other two branches are elected by popular vote of the Cherokee Nation.

Skill 3.2   Identify major concepts, content, and purposes of the U.S. Constitution and other historical documents.

The Constitution of the United States established the three branches of the federal government., The **Executive**, the **Legislative**, and the **Judicial**, divide the powers of the federal government thus:

Legislative – Article 1 of the Constitution established the legislative, or law-making branch of the government called the Congress. It is made up of two houses, the House of Representatives and the Senate. Voters in all states elect the members who serve in each respective House of Congress. The legislative branch is responsible for making laws, raising and printing money, regulating trade, establishing the postal service and federal courts, approving the President's appointments, declaring war and supporting the armed forces. The Congress also has the power to *impeach* (bring charges against) the President. Charges for impeachment are brought by the House of Representatives, and are then tried in the Senate.

Executive – Article 2 of the Constitution created the executive branch of the government, headed by the President, who leads the country, recommends new laws, and can veto bills passed by the legislative branch. As the chief of state, the President is responsible for carrying out the laws of the country and the treaties and declarations of war passed by the legislative branch. The President also appoints federal judges and is commander-in-chief of the military. Other members of the executive branch include the Vice-President, also elected, and various cabinet members as he might appoint: ambassadors, presidential advisors, members of the armed forces, and other appointed and civil servants of government agencies, departments and bureaus. Though the President appoints them, they must be approved by the legislative branch.

Judicial – Article 3 of the Constitution established the judicial branch of government headed by the Supreme Court. The Supreme Court has the power to rule that a law passed by the legislature, or an act of the executive branch is illegal and unconstitutional. Citizens, businesses, and government officials can also, in an appeal capacity, ask the Supreme Court to review a decision made in a lower court if someone believes that the ruling by a judge is unconstitutional. The judicial branch also includes lower federal courts known as federal district courts that have been established by the Congress.

Powers delegated to the federal government: Powers reserved to the states:

1. To tax.
2. To borrow and coin money
3. To establish postal service.
4. To grant patents and copyrights.
5. To regulate interstate/foreign commerce.
6. To establish courts.
7. To declare war.
8. To raise and support the armed forces.
9. To govern territories.
10. To define and punish felonies and piracy on the high seas.
11. To fix standards of weights and measures.
12. To conduct foreign affairs.

1. To regulate intrastate trade.
2. To establish local govts.
3. To protect general welfare.
4. To protect life and property.
5. To ratify amendments.
6. To conduct elections.
7. To make state and local laws.

Concurrent powers of the federal government and states.

1. Both Congress and the states may tax.
2. Both may borrow money.
3. Both may charter banks and corporations.
4. Both may establish courts.
5. Both may make and enforce laws.
6. Both may take property for public purposes.
7. Both may spend money to provide for the public welfare.

<u>Implied powers of the federal government</u>.

1. To establish banks or other corporations, implied from delegated powers to tax, borrow, and to regulate commerce.
2. To spend money for roads, schools, health, insurance, etc. implied from powers to establish post roads, to tax to provide for general welfare and defense, and to regulate commerce.
3. To create military academies, implied from powers to raise and support an armed force.
4. To locate and generate sources of power and sell surplus, implied from powers to dispose of government property, commerce, and war powers.
5. To assist and regulate agriculture, implied from power to tax and spend for general welfare and regulate commerce.

Skill 3.3   Compare and contrast the various political systems in the world (e.g., monarchy, parliamentary system, federal republic, democracy, totalitarianism).

Authoritarian governments, common throughout history, still exist today, mostly in the form of communist societies, like China. In this form of government, all the members of the government belong to one political party; in China's case, it is the Communist Party. Not all members of the government believe the same on small issues, but significant issues require party unity. Organization of alternative political parties is widely and strongly discouraged. This was the case in the Soviet Union, the best-known communist state, which disappeared in 1991. Also in many authoritarian governments, industries exist to produce revenues for the state. The flip side of this is that the government is responsible for the upkeep and outlays for these industries. This was much more the case in the Soviet Union than it is in China today, but certain elements of authoritarianism pervade Chinese society to this day.

The most familiar form of government to most Westerners is the **representative government**, commonly called a republic or democracy. The idea behind this form of government is that the people in a society are ultimately responsible for their government and the laws that it passes, enforces, and interprets in that they, the people, elect many of the members of that government. The members of a representative government are much more aware of public opinion than their authoritarian-government counterparts, although too much oppression can drive a desperate people to revolt, as has been done many times in the past, including in the U.S.

The representative government began, in Western tradition, in Greece, with democracy, then progressed to the republic in Rome and on into other democracies and republics, most famously the United States and many other countries around the world. These governments are termed **democracies** by many, but they are more properly called **republics**. A democracy involves *everyone* in a society having a say in who is elected to that society's government.

This is certainly not the case in the U.S., in which not only does everyone not vote but also not everyone *can* vote. Another main difference between a true democracy and the kind of democracy that the U.S. and other countries are called these days is that in a true democracy, a vote on anything can be called at any time.

Types of governments and philosophies:

Anarchism - Political movement believing in the elimination of all government and its replacement by a cooperative community of individuals. Sometimes it has involved political violence such as assassinations of important political or governmental figures. The historical banner of the movement is a black flag.

Communism - A belief as well as a political system, characterized by the ideology of class conflict and revolution, one party state and dictatorship, repressive police apparatus, and government ownership of the means of production and distribution of goods and services. A revolutionary ideology preaching the eventual overthrow of all other political orders and the establishment of one world Communist government. Same as Marxism. The historical banner of the movement is a red flag and variation of stars, hammer and sickles, representing the various types of workers.

Dictatorship - The rule by an individual or small group of individuals (Oligarchy) that centralizes all political control in itself and enforces its will with a terrorist police force.

Fascism - A belief as well as a political system, opposed ideologically to Communism, though similar in basic structure, with a one party state, centralized political control and a repressive police system. It however tolerates private ownership of the means of production, though it maintains tight overall control. Central to its belief is the idolization of the Leader, a "Cult of the Personality," and most often an expansionist ideology. Examples have been German Nazism and Italian Fascism.

Monarchy - The rule of a nation by a Monarch, (a non-elected usually hereditary leader), most often a king or queen. It may or may not be accompanied by some measure of democratic open institutions and elections at various levels. A modern example is Great Britain, where it is called a Constitutional Monarchy.

Parliamentary System - A system of government with a legislature, usually involving a multiplicity of political parties and often coalition politics. There is division between the head of state and head of government. Head of government is usually known as a Prime Minister who is also usually the head of the largest party. The head of government and cabinet usually both sit and vote in the parliament. Head of state is most often an elected president, (though in the case of a constitutional monarchy, like Great Britain, the sovereign may take the place of a president as head of state). A government may fall when a majority in parliament votes "no confidence" in the government.

Presidential System - A system of government with a legislature, can involve few or many political parties, no division between head of state and head of government. The President serves in both capacities. The President is elected either by direct or indirect election. A President and cabinet usually do not sit or vote in the legislature and the President may or may not be the head of the largest political party. A President can thus rule even without a majority in the legislature. He can only be removed from office before an election for major infractions of the law.

Socialism - Political belief and system in which the state takes a guiding role in the national economy and provides extensive social services to its population. It may or may not own outright means of production, but even where it does not, it exercises tight control. It usually promotes democracy, (Democratic-Socialism), though the heavy state involvement produces excessive bureaucracy and usually inefficiency. Taken to an extreme it may lead to Communism as government control increases and democratic practice decreases. Ideologically the two movements are very similar in both belief and practice, as Socialists also preach the superiority of their system to all others and that it will become the eventual natural order. It is also considered for that reason a variant of Marxism. It also has used a red flag as a symbol.

Skill 3.4 Identify the characteristics of the U.S. electoral system and the election process.

The term **suffrage** means voting or the right to vote. Historically the right to vote has always been very limited. Elections have always been associated with democratic practices but various limitations have been placed on the right to vote throughout history. These have included property qualifications, poll taxes, residency requirements, and restrictions against the right of women to vote.

In 1787, the Constitution of the United States provided for the election of the chief executive in Article II, Section I, and members of the national legislature in Article I, Section II. A number of election abuses, however, led to the adoption of what was known as the Australian, or secret, ballot and the practice of registering voters prior to Election Day. Voting machines were first used in the United States in 1892. During the 19th century, the electorate in the United States grew considerably, most of the states franchised all white male adults, although the so-called poll tax was retained. (It was abolished by the 24th Amendment to the Constitution, ratified in 1964.) The 15th Amendment to the United States Constitution ratified in 1870, extended the vote to the former black slaves. In the period after the Civil War, known as Reconstruction, many blacks were elected to high office for the first time in American history. It was during the post-Civil War period that the primary system of selecting candidates for public office became widely used. By 1900, the system of primaries was regulated by law in most states. Women in the United States were granted the right to vote by the 19th Amendment to the Constitution which was ratified in 1920. The right to vote was extended to those eighteen years of age by the 26th Amendment to the Constitution in 1971.

The struggle over what is to be the fair method to ensure equal political representation for all different groups in the United States continues to dominate the national debate. This has revolved around the problems of trying to ensure proper racial and minority representation. Various civil rights acts, notable the **Voting Rights Act of 1965**, sought to eliminate the remaining features of unequal suffrage in the United States.

Recently the question has revolved around the issue of "Gerrymandering", which involves the adjustment of various electoral districts in order to achieve a predetermined goal. Usually this is used in regards to the problem of minority political representation. The fact that this sometimes creates odd and unusual looking districts, (this is where the practice gets its name), and most often the sole basis of the adjustments is racial, has led to the questioning of this practice being a fair and constitutional, way for society to achieve its desired goals. The Supreme Court determined in 2006 that an instance of gerrymandering in Texas to ensure the election of a certain conservative Republican congressmen was legal.

Skill 3.5   **Identify the major structures and functions of federal, state, and local governments in the United States.**

See Skill 3.2

Skill 3.6   Analyze relationships between social, cultural, economic, and political institutions and systems.

Forms of Government are listed below:

Anarchism - Political movement believing in the elimination of all government and its replacement by a cooperative community of individuals. Sometimes it has involved political violence such as assassinations of important political or governmental figures. The historical banner of the movement is a black flag.

Communism - A belief, as well as a political system, characterized by the ideology of class conflict and revolution, one party state and dictatorship, repressive police apparatus, and government ownership of the means of production and distribution of goods and services. Communism supports a revolutionary ideology preaching the eventual overthrow of all other political orders and the establishment of one world communist government. The historical banner of the movement is a red flag with a variation of stars and hammer and sickles, representing the various types of workers.

Dictatorship - The rule by an individual or small elite group of individuals (oligarchy) that centralizes all political control in itself. A dictator may enforce his will with a terrorist police force.

Fascism - A belief, as well as a political system, opposed ideologically to Communism, though similar in basic structure with a one-party state, centralized political control, and a repressive police system. It however tolerates private ownership of the means of production though it maintains tight overall control. Central to its belief is the idolization of the leader, a "Cult of the Personality," and most often an expansionist ideology. Examples have been German Nazism and Italian Fascism.

Monarchy - The rule of a nation by a monarch (a non-elected, usually hereditary leader), a king, queen, emperor, empress. It may or may not be accompanied by some measure of democratic open institutions and elections at various levels. A modern example is Great Britain, where it is called a constitutional monarchy.

Parliamentary System - A system of government with a legislature that usually involves a multiplicity of political parties--and often coalition politics. There is division between the head of state and head of government. Head of government is usually known as a Prime Minister who is usually the head of the largest party. The head of government and cabinet usually both sit and vote in the parliament. Head of state is most often an elected president (though in the case of a constitutional monarchy like Great Britain, the sovereign may take the place of a president as head of state). A government may fall when a majority in parliament votes "no confidence" in the government.

Presidential System - A system of government with a legislature can involve few or many political parties with no division between head of state and head of government. The President serves in both capacities. The President is elected either by direct or indirect election. A president and cabinet usually do not sit or vote in the legislature, and the president may or may not be the head of the largest political party. A president can thus rule even without a majority in the legislature. He can only be removed from office before an election for major infractions of the law.

Socialism - Political belief and system in which the state takes a guiding role in the national economy and provides extensive social services to its population. It may or may not own outright means of production, but even where it does not, it exercises tight control. It usually promotes democracy (Democratic Socialism), though the heavy state involvement produces excessive bureaucracy and usually inefficiency. Taken to an extreme, it may lead to Communism as government control increases and democratic practice decreases. Ideologically the two movements are very similar in both belief and practice, as Socialists also preach the superiority of their system to all others and that it will become the eventual natural order. It is also considered for that reason a variant of Marxism. It has used a red flag as a symbol.

The differences between **democracy** vs. **totalitarianism** and **authoritarianism** are an easy contrast to draw. The differences between totalitarianism and authoritarianism are not as readily apparent. Authoritarianism exists on different levels and can exist in all forms of government, at least to some extent. In the United States, for example, authoritarianism exists on some points for national security. But an authoritarian government is usually undemocratic, and the rulers do not need the consent of those they are governing. Totalitarianism (derived from the word *total*) is the extreme form of authoritarianism. Totalitarianism depends on authoritarianism to function. While an authoritarian regime will tolerate some pluralism; the totalitarian regime will not. The main difference between totalitarianism and authoritarianism is that totalitarianism is guided by an ideology.

Thus the totalitarian government sees itself as having a legitimate concern with all levels of human existence—not only in regard to speech or press, but even to social and religious institutions. It tries to achieve a complete conformity to its ideals. As Benito Mussolini said: "Nothing outside of the state, nothing instead of the state."

Regimes that conform to the **authoritarianism** can be seen throughout history. This model can be seen in the history of Central and South America, where regimes, usually representing the interests of the upper classes, came to power and instituted dictatorships that seek to concentrate all political power in a few hands. The Catholic Church in this region became an institution of opposition to the state authority.

Democracy is a much more familiar system to us because in the United States, it is the system under which we live. The term comes from the Greek "for the rule of the people." The two most prevalent types are **direct** and **indirect** democracy. Direct democracy functions when the population involved is relatively small and will usually involve all the voters in a given area coming together to vote and decide on issues that will affect them, such as the town meeting in New England. An **indirect democracy** involves much larger areas and populations and involves the sending of representatives to a legislative body to vote on issues affecting the people. Such a system can be comprised of a **Presidential** or **Parliamentary** system. In the United States, we follow an indirect—or representative—democracy.

Skill 3.7   Identify the tenets (e.g., rule of law, innocent until proven guilty), institutions, and processes of the U.S. legal system.

The terms "civil liberties" and "civil rights" are often used interchangeably, but there are some fine distinctions between the two terms. The term "civil liberties" refers to how people's freedoms are protected from government's abuse of power with restrictions set on how much that government can interfere with the lives of the people. The American Civil Liberties Union (ACLU) defends certain "civil liberties" that some do not believe should be civil liberties. "Civil rights" identifies equality and includes laws that prohibit private businesses, etc., from discriminating against individuals.

Although the term "civil rights" has thus been identified with the ideal of equality and the term "civil liberties" with the idea of freedom, the two concepts are really inseparable and interacting. Equality implies the proper ordering of liberty in a society so that one individual's freedom does not infringe on the rights of others.

The beginnings of civil liberties and the idea of civil rights in the United States go back to the ideas of the Greeks. The experience of the early British struggles for civil rights and to the very philosophies that led people to come to the New World in the first place. Religious freedom, political freedom, and the right to live one's life as one sees fit are basic to the American ideal. These were embodied in the ideas expressed in the Declaration of Independence and the Constitution.

All these ideas found their final expression in the United States Constitution's first ten amendments, known as the **Bill of Rights**. In 1789, the first Congress passed these first amendments and by December 1791, three-fourths of the states at that time had ratified them. The Bill of Rights protects certain liberties and basic rights. James Madison expressed that the majority rules the minority but that the minority needs to be protected against the majority. The Bill of Rights protects people and prevents government and others from taking away these rights.

To summarize:

The first amendment guarantees the basic rights of freedom of religion, freedom of speech, freedom of the press, and freedom of assembly.

The next three amendments came out of the colonists' struggle with Great Britain. For example, the third amendment prevents Congress from forcing citizens to keep troops in their homes. Before the Revolution, Great Britain tried to coerce the colonists to house soldiers. The second amendment guarantees the right to bear arms, and the fourth amendment protects against unreasonable search.

Amendments five through eight protect citizens who are accused of crimes and are brought to trial. Every citizen has the right to due process of law (due process being that the government must follow the same fair rules for everyone brought to trial. These rules include the right to a trial by an impartial jury, the right to be defended by a lawyer, and the right to a speedy trial.

The last two amendments limit the powers of the federal government to those that are expressly granted in the Constitution; thus, any rights not expressly mentioned in the Constitution belong to the states or to the people.

In regards to specific guarantees:

Freedom of Religion: Religious freedom has not been seriously threatened in the United States. The policy of the government has been guided by the premise that church and state should be separate. But when religious practices have been at cross purposes with prevailing attitudes or mores in the nation at particular times, restrictions have been placed on certain practices. Some of these have been restrictions against the practice of polygamy that is supported by certain religious groups. The idea of animal sacrifice that is promoted by some religious beliefs is generally prohibited. The use of mind-altering, illegal substances that some use in religious rituals has been restricted. In the United States, all recognized religious institutions are tax-exempt in following the idea of separation of church and state. Unfortunately, there have been quasi-religious groups that have tried to take advantage of this fact. All of these issues continue, and most likely will continue to occupy both political and legal considerations for some time to come.

Freedom of Speech, Press, and Assembly: These rights historically have been given wide latitude in their practices although there have been instances when these rights are limited for various reasons. The classic limitation, for instance, in regards to freedom of speech was stated by Supreme Justice Oliver Wendall Holmes: "The question in every case is whether the words used are used in such circumstances and are of such a nature as to create a clear and present danger that they will bring about the substantive evils that Congress has a right to prevent." Under **Brandenburg v. Ohio**, it was ruled that government cannot punish inflammatory speech unless it is directed to inciting and likely to incite imminent lawless action.

There is also a prohibition against **slander**, the intentional *stating* of a deliberate falsehood against one party by another, and **libel**, the *printing* of a known falsehood. In times of national emergency, various restrictions have been placed on the rights of press, speech—and sometimes assembly. Pornography is subject to law.

America has a number of organizations that put themselves out as champions of the fight for civil liberties and civil rights in this country, the ACLU for example. Much criticism, however, has been raised at times against these groups as to whether or not they are really protecting rights or liberties or are attempting to create "new" rights.

"Rights" come with a measure of responsibility and respect for the public order, all of which must be taken into consideration.

Overall, the American experience has been one of exemplary conduct regarding the protection of individual rights, but there too has been a lag in its practice—notably the refusal to grant full and equal rights to blacks, the very fact of their enslavement, and the second class status of women for much of American history. Yet, the country has proved itself to be largely able to change when it has not lived up to its stated ideals.

Though much effort and suffering accompanied the civil rights struggle, for example, in the end the struggle did succeed in changing the basic foundation of society profoundly. America continues its commitment to a strong tradition of freedom and liberty that was, and is, the underlying feature of American society.

How best to move forward ensuring civil liberties and civil rights for all continues to dominate the national debate. Recently, issues that seem to revolve not around individual rights, but what has been called "group rights" have been raised. At the forefront of the debate is whether some specific remedies including affirmative action, quotas, gerrymandering (redistricting), and various other forms of preferential treatment are actually fair or just as bad as the ills they are supposed to cure. At the present no easy answers seem to be forthcoming. It is a testament to the American system that it has shown itself able to enter into these debates to find solutions and then tends to come out stronger.

The fact that the United States has the longest single constitutional history in the modern era is just one reason to be optimistic about the future of American liberty.

Skill 3.8   Identify major U.S. Supreme Court cases and their impact on society.

The Bill of Rights consists of the first ten Amendments to the U.S. Constitution. These amendments were passed almost immediately upon ratification of the Constitution by the states. They reflect the concerns that were raised throughout the country and by the Founding Fathers during the ratification process. These Amendments reflect the fears and concerns of the people that the power and authority of the government be restricted from denying or limiting the rights of the people of the nation. The experiences of the founders of the nation as colonists formed the foundation of the concern to limit the power of government.

The Bill of Rights has been interpreted in different ways at different times by different interpreters. These, and other, Constitutional Amendments may be interpreted very strictly or very loosely. The terms of the amendments may be defined in different way to enfranchise or to disenfranchise individuals or groups of persons.

Example: During and after Reconstruction, the interpretation of the Bill of Rights that did not include blacks in the definition of a citizen necessitated the passage of the 14th and 15th amendments. The interpretation of these amendments was broadly interpreted by the Supreme Court in the Plessey case, resulting in the establishment of the doctrine of "separate but equal." It was not until fifty years later, in the case of Brown v. Board of Education, that a narrower interpretation of the amendment resulted in a Supreme Court decision that reversed the previous interpretation.

Effects of the Court's interpretations of the Constitution

Marbury v. Madison is perhaps the most famous Supreme Court case of them all. It was the first case to establish what has become the Court's main duty, judicial review.

After George Washington retired, his vice-president, John Adams, succeeded him. Adams ran for election in 1800, and was opposed by his vice-president, Thomas Jefferson. Adams was a Federalist. Jefferson was elected in November 1800. At that time, the new president didn't take office until March 4 of the following year. So Adams had a few months to try to get things done before Jefferson took over. One of the things Adams tried to do was get as many Federalist judges appointed as he could. As March 4 drew near, Adams got more and more concerned with doing this. He kept appointing judges long into the night on March 3. These were known as the "**Midnight Judges**." One of these "Midnight Judges" was **William Marbury**, who was named to be justice of the peace for the District of Columbia.

The normal practice of making such appointments was to deliver a "**commission**," or notice, of appointment. This was normally done by the Secretary of State. Jefferson's Secretary of State at the time was **James Madison**. Jefferson didn't want all those Federalist judges, so he told Madison not to deliver the commission. Marshall and the rest of the Supreme Court decided that the power to deliver commissions to judges, since it was part of the Judiciary Act of 1789 and not part of the Constitution itself, was in conflict with the Constitution and, therefore, illegal. Further, the entire Judiciary Act of 1789 was illegal because it gave to the Judicial Branch powers not granted to it by the Constitution.

It appeared that Marshall sided with his political enemies, but this was not the case. Marbury, a Federalist, didn't get to be Justice of the Peace in the District of Columbia. Adams was probably quite angry because his commission was denied. Jefferson and Madison were probably quite happy because they got to name their own friendly justice of the peace. But Marshall gave to the Supreme Court a whole new power: the power to throw out laws of Congress. So, no matter how many laws Thomas Jefferson and his Democratic-Republicans passed and made into law, the Supreme Court always had the ultimate check on that legislative and executive power. John Marshall, in appearing to lose the political battle, won the political war.

One of the chief political battles of the nineteenth century was between the federal government and state governments. The Supreme Court took this battle to heart and issued a series of decisions that, for the most part, made it clear that any dispute between governments at the state and federal levels would be settled in favor of the federal government. One of the main examples of this was *McCulloch v. Maryland,* which settled a dispute involving the Bank of the United States.

The United States, at this time (1819) still had a federal bank, the Bank of the United States. The State of Maryland voted to tax all bank business not done with state banks. This was meant to be a tax on people who lived in Maryland but who did business with banks in other states. However, the State of Maryland also sought to tax the federal bank. Andrew McCulloch, who worked in the Baltimore branch of the Bank of the United States, refused to pay the tax. The State of Maryland sued, and the Supreme Court accepted the case.

Writing for the Court, Chief Justice John Marshall wrote that the federal government did indeed have the right and power to set up a federal bank. Further, he wrote, a state did not have the power to tax the federal government. "The right to tax is the right to destroy," he wrote, and states should not have that power over the federal government. The Bank of the United States did not survive, but the judicial review of the Supreme Court did.

The Supreme Court reasserted the power of judicial review in **United States v. Nixon**, one of the most dynamic and divisive of the twentieth century. The issue was whether the President had the ability to keep certain items secret. In this case, the items were secret recordings that Richard Nixon, the President at the time, had made of conversations he had had with his advisers. The recordings were thought to implicate Nixon in the cover-up of the Watergate break-in, an attempt by a team of thieves to gain information on the activities of George McGovern, Nixon's opponent in the 1972 election. Nixon claimed that the tapes were the property of the Executive Branch and, more to the point, of Nixon himself. Nixon claimed an "executive privilege" that would keep him from having to relinquish the recordings.

The real issue, though, was that the recordings had been subpoenaed by the Judicial Branch. Thus, the dispute was really whether the Judicial Branch could supersede the authority of the Executive Branch. Like John Marshall before him, Chief Justice Warren Burger declared that the Judicial Branch could trump both other branches in its pursuit of justice and that *no one*, not even the President, was above the law.

Controversies that have resulted over the interpretations of civil rights

Civil rights came to the fore in a big way with the infamous **Dred Scott v. Sanford** case, in which the Supreme Court famously declared that Scott, a former slave, had no rights even though he was free of his former master. The Civil War changed public opinion, at least in the North, but the struggle for African-Americans especially to achieve basic rights like voting and owning property continued to varying degrees throughout the nineteenth and twentieth centuries.

The court built on the Dred Scott model in 1883, with *The Civil Rights Cases*, a series of five decisions that said, in essence, that the newly minted Fourteenth Amendment and its equal protection clause didn't apply to private individuals or their companies. Little more than a decade later, the Court expanded its denial of the equal protection clause in the infamous **Plessy v. Ferguson** (1896), in which "separate but equal" railway cars were deemed appropriate and legal. The Plessy decision was even more wide-reaching in its ramifications because it applied to state-run organizations. That right to discriminate was extended to schools in 1908 (*Berea College* v. *Kentucky*), and the segregation movement was off and running at high speed.

African-Americans responded with activism and positivism. Led by such public and successful groups as the Universal Negro Improvement Association and the NAACP, African-Americans began to speak out in favor of rights that they were denied in the court of law and in everyday public life. Decades of activism followed and the "separate but equal" doctrine was thrown under more scrutiny.

These activist efforts very often met with virulent opposition, extending to violence in many cases. The Court, ever mindful of public opinion, looked for an opportunity to try to reverse legalized segregation and found it in *Brown* v. *Board of Education*. It was a unanimous decision, and it overturned *Plessy* in ruling that "separate but equal facilities were inherently unequal." It was only the beginning, and at first it applied only to public schools; but the end of legalized segregation had begun. Efforts to hold on to it continued (most famously at Little Rock Central High in 1957), and subsequent Court decisions weren't exactly stern in their rebukes of the various states' (especially Southern) slow speed for complying with those decisions. Still, the efforts continued, and so did the legal support for them. Wide-ranging protests followed, including freedom marches, sit-ins at lunch counters, Freedom Rides, and riots. The Court continued to support desegregation, to varying degrees, and the foot-dragging in the South eventually stopped.

In recent years, however, the phrase "**race-neutral**" has begun to be used. This term seems to be being applied more and more as a response to affirmative action programs, which attempted to grant preferences to African-Americans in order to make up for past injustices. One of the most famous of these series of events culminated in *Regents of the University of California* v. *Bakke* (1978), in which the Court invalidated the denial of a white student from law school because the school had to meet its mandated quota of minority applicants. In 1995, in *Adarand Constructors, Inc.* v. *Pena*, the Court mandated that race neutrality be examined in federal agencies under "**strict scrutiny**"; in effect, the Court had validated the idea of race neutrality and ended the raft of affirmative action programs that had dotted the federal government's departments and agencies.

Along with the idea of the government lending a helping hand to those struggling for basic civil rights came the idea of aiding those who were facing a daunting path through the legal system. Prisoners, especially non-white ones, didn't have a whole lot of rights under the law or certainly in practice. The one Court case that resonates throughout the latter half of the twentieth century is *Miranda v. Arizona*, in which the Court set out a series of information that arresting officers had to impart to those they were arresting, including such Bill of Rights-friendly language as the right to an attorney, the right to avoid self-incrimination, and the right to a trial by jury. Other law enforcement cases preceded it and followed it, with the idea that a person who is arrested has the presumption of innocence until guilt has been proven.

Perhaps the most wide-ranging yet personal civil rights case to come about in the last decade is **Bush** v. **Palm Beach County Canvassing Board**. Presidential candidate George W. Bush sued to invalidate the recount that had begun in the wake of Bush's narrow victory over Al Gore in Florida. Bush claimed, among other things, that his Fifth Amendment due process rights were violated by the various decisions made in the wake of the close vote counts. The result was a decision by the Court to stop all recounting and declare Bush the winner. This was not a classical civil rights case, per se, but it was one that argued as such and involved the sort of protection that had been argued under previous Fifth and Fourteenth Amendment cases.

Skill 3.9   Evaluate the goals, conduct, and consequences of U.S. foreign policy.

There are many theories of international relations, all of which seek to describe how sovereign countries interact, or should interact, with one another. Four of the primary schools of thought in international theory are Realism, Liberalism, Institutionalism and Constructivism.

Realism is an international theory that holds the nation-state as the basic unit and recognizes no international authority above individual nations. Realism is based on the assumption that nations act only in their own self interest to preserve their own security. Realism holds that international relations are based on the relative military and economic power between nations, and that nations are inherently aggressive.

Liberalism is often thought of as being opposed to realism in philosophy. Instead of assuming that states only act in their own interest, liberalism allows for the cooperation of several states working in common interest. Instead of the Realist belief that states act based on their capabilities, Liberalism holds that states act based on their preferences. The term Liberalism was first used critically by Realist thinkers to describe the international theories of Woodrow Wilson.

Institutionalism is a theory of international relations that holds that there is a structure to the interactions of nations that determines how they will act. The rules that nations follow in making international decisions are called institutions. Institutions can give structure, distribute power, and provide incentives for international cooperation.

Constructivism is similar to Liberalism in philosophy but recognizes the role that ideas and perceptions play in international relations. Constructivism makes note of traditional relations between countries and their relative goals, identities and perceived threats. Constructivism recognizes, for instance, that a country building up its military is likely to be taken as more of a threat by that country's traditional antagonists than by its allies.

In practice, international relations are often conducted through **diplomacy.**

Nations that formally recognize one another, station a group of diplomats, led by an ambassador, in one another's countries to provide formal representation on international matters. Diplomats convey official information on the policies and positions of their home countries to the host countries where they are stationed. Diplomats are also involved in negotiating international agreements on issues such as trade, environmental issues, and conflict resolutions. Countries sometimes engage in informal diplomacy between private individuals when they wish to discuss common issues without taking official positions.

Diplomacy also takes place within international organizations such as the United Nations. Member nations send diplomatic representation to the U.N. and have input into forming international policy. While member countries agree to abide by U.N. resolutions as a condition of membership, in practice there is often dissent. The U.N. has the ability to impose economic and other sanctions on its members for failing to follow its decisions, but other types of enforcement have been problematic. The U.N. has the ability to raise military forces from its member countries; however, these forces have historically been limited to peacekeeping missions, not active military campaigns.

Skill 3.10   Identify features and concepts of international relations (e.g., United Nations, Organization of the Petroleum Exporting Countries, Red Cross, Organization of American States, European Union).

With the emergence of so many new independent nations after World War II, the role of **international organizations** such as the newly formed United Nations grew in importance. The United Nations was formed after World War II to establish peaceful ties between countries. Dismayed by the failure of the former League of Nations to prevent war, the organizers of the United Nations provided for the ability to deploy peacekeeping troops and to impose sanctions and restrictions on member states. Other international organizations arose to take the place of former colonial connections. The British Commonwealth and the French Union, for example, maintained connections between Britain and France and their former colonies.

The goals, structures, and functions of the United Nations

The **United Nations** (U.N.) is an international organization headquartered in New York City. The U.N. was founded in 1945. Representatives of 51 countries signed the original agreement. More and more countries have joined since then, and membership now includes 192 countries.

At the top of the U.N. hierarchy is the Security Council, a group that has 15 members. Five of these are permanent members and can veto any U.N. resolution. The permanent members are the United States, United Kingdom, France, China, and Russia. The other ten members are elected for two-year terms, with five being elected each year.

The General Assembly is the only organization that has every member nation represented. Each country sends one person to officially represent it in the General Assembly, which meets regularly at U.N. Headquarters in New York. Special sessions of the General Assembly are rare but not unheard of.

Perhaps the most well known U.N. figure is the **Secretary General** who acts as the administrative head of the entire U.N. He or she is the spokesperson for the U.N. The Secretary General serves a five-year term and can be re-elected, by the General Assembly. By tradition, the Secretary General is not from a nation that is a permanent member of the Security Council. The Secretary General is the head of the Secretariat, another important U.N. body that exists mainly to support the inner workings of the General Assembly.

Another of the major organizations within the U.N. is the International Court of Justice, which has its headquarters in The Hague, the Netherlands. This court is responsible for trying people suspected of international crimes.

One of the prime functions of the United Nations is to keep peace throughout the world. Member nations send a large number of armed forces on a rotating basis to the U.N. Peacekeeping Force, which sends troops to armed conflicts or violent situations. This peacekeeping extends to elections, and U.N. peacekeepers have both observed and enforced free practices for elections across the globe.

Related to the peacekeeping mission of the U.N. is its pursuit of human rights. Genocide and other examples of inhumanity are not tolerated, and U.N. members work tirelessly to discourage such efforts, including sending armed troops to stop them. The U.N. has a Universal Declaration of Human Rights to support this and several other high-profile organizations, including the United Nations Children's Fund (UNICEF) and the World Health Organization (WHO). U.N. workers have led humanitarian efforts around the world, delivering food and liquids to famine-stricken areas.

International political borders and territorial sovereignty in a global economy

GATT, NAFTA, WTO and EU are all forms of **trade liberalization**. The **GATT** or **General Agreements on Tariffs and Trade** was founded in 1947 and today, as the **World Trade Organization** or **WTO**, has 147 member nations. It was based on three principles. The first was Most Favored National status for all members. This means trade based on comparative advantage without tariffs or trade barriers. The second principle was elimination of quotas and third, reduction of trade barriers through multi-lateral trade negotiations. The WTO is the successor to the GATT and came into being in 1995. Its objective is to promote free trade. As such it administers trade agreements, settles disputes, and provides a forum for trade discussions and negotiations.

The **North American Free Trade Agreement** or **NAFTA** and the **EU** are both forms of regional economic integration. Economic integration is a method of trade liberalization on a regional basis. NAFTA represents the lowest form or first step in the regional trade integration process. A **free trade area** consists for two or more countries that abolish tariffs and other trade barriers among themselves but maintain their own trade barriers against the rest of the world. A free trade area allows for specialization and trade on the basis of comparative advantage within the area. The next stage in the integration process is a customs union, which is a free trade area that has common external tariffs against non-members. The third stage is a common market which is a customs union with free factor mobility within the area. Factors migrate where they find the best payment within the area. The fourth state is economic union where the common market members have common or coordinated economic and social policies. The final stage is monetary union where the area has a common currency. This is what Europe is working toward. They have a common market with elements of the fourth and fifth stages of integration.

The WTO does not change or blur the significance of political borders and territorial sovereignty in the same way that economic integration does, although the WTO is a way of settling trade disputes that arise from the different integration agreements. In the advanced stages of economic integration the political borders remain, but economic and social policies are common or coordinated and in monetary union, there is one common currency. Each nation is its own independent entity but they give up some sovereignty in the interest of having a successful union.

Trade agreements proliferate in the world today. The Smoot Hawley Tariffs and the rounds of retaliation in the 1930s are what laid the basis for what today are the WTO and the European Union (EU). The GATT and the beginnings of what is now the EU came into being as organizations trying to undo the effects of the Great Depression and the world war. Free trade without trade barriers results in the most efficient use of resources, with higher consumption, employment and income levels for all participants. This is why there are so many free trade agreements being negotiated in today's world.

Skill 3.11   Identify the rights and responsibilities of a U.S. citizen in society.

The terms "civil liberties" and "civil rights" are often used interchangeably, but there are some fine distinctions between the two terms. The term civil liberties is more often used to imply that the state has a positive role to play in assuring that all its' citizens will have equal protection and justice under the law with equal opportunities to exercise their privileges of citizenship and to participate fully in the life of the nation, regardless of race, religion, sex, color or creed. The term civil rights is used more often to refer to rights that may be described as guarantees that are specified as against the state authority implying limitations on the actions of the state to interfere with citizens' liberties. Although the term "civil rights" has thus been identified with the ideal of equality and the term "civil liberties" with the idea of freedom, the two concepts are really inseparable and interacting. Equality implies the proper ordering of liberty in a society so that one individual's freedom does not infringe on the rights of others.

The beginnings of civil liberties and the idea of civil rights in the United States go back to the ideas of the Greeks. Also the experience of the early British struggle for civil rights and to the very philosophies that led people to come to the New World in the first place. Religious freedom, political freedom, and the right to live one's life as one sees fit are basic to the American ideal. These were embodied in the ideas expressed in the Declaration of Independence and the Constitution.

All these ideas found their final expression in the United States Constitution's first ten amendments, known as the **Bill of Rights**. In 1789, the first Congress passed these first amendments and by December, 1791, three-fourths of the states at that time had ratified them. The Bill of Rights protects certain liberties and basic rights. James Madison who wrote the amendments said that the Bill of Rights does not give Americans these rights. People, Madison said, already have these rights. They are natural rights that belong to all human beings. The Bill of Rights simply prevents the governments from taking away these rights.

To summarize:

The first amendment guarantees the basic rights of freedom of religion, freedom of speech, freedom of the press, and freedom of assembly.

The next three amendments came out of the colonists' struggle with Great Britain. For example, the third amendment prevents Congress from forcing citizens to keep troops in their homes. Before the Revolution, Great Britain tried to coerce the colonists to house soldiers.

Amendments five through eight protect citizens who are accused of crimes and are brought to trial. Every citizen has the right to due process of law, (due process as defined earlier, being that the government must follow the same fair rules for everyone brought to trial.) These rules include the right to a trial by an impartial jury, the right to be defended by a lawyer, and the right to a speedy trial. The last two amendments limit the powers of the federal government to those that are expressly granted in the Constitution, any rights not expressly mentioned in the Constitution, thus, belong to the states or to the people.

In regards to specific guarantees:

Freedom of Religion: Religious freedom has not been seriously threatened in the United States historically. The policy of the government has been guided by the premise that church and state should be separate. But when religious practices have been at cross purposes with attitudes prevailing in the nation at particular times, there has been restrictions placed on these practices. Some of these have been restrictions against the practice of polygamy that is supported by certain religious groups. The idea of animal sacrifice that is promoted by some religious beliefs is generally prohibited. The use of mind altering illegal substances that some use in religious rituals has been restricted. In the United States, all recognized religious institutions are tax-exempt in following the idea of separation of church and state, and therefore, there have been many quasi-religious groups that have in the past tried to take advantage of this fact. All of these issues continue, and most likely will continue to occupy both political and legal considerations for some time to come.

Freedom of Speech, Press, and Assembly: These rights historically have been given wide latitude in their practices, though there has been instances when one or the other have been limited for various reasons. The most classic limitation, for instance, in regards to freedom of speech, has been the famous precept that an individual is prohibited from yelling fire! in a crowded theatre. This prohibition is an example of the state saying that freedom of speech does not extend to speech that might endanger other people. There is also a prohibition against **slander,** or the knowingly stating of a deliberate falsehood against one party by another. Also there are many regulations regarding freedom of the press, the most common example are the various laws against **libel,** (or the printing of a known falsehood). In times of national emergency, various restrictions have been placed on the rights of press, speech and sometimes assembly.

The legal system in recent years has also undergone a number of serious changes, some would say challenges, with the interpretation of some constitutional guarantees.

America also has a number of organizations that put themselves out as champions of the fight for civil liberties and civil rights in this country. Much criticism, however, has been raised at times against these groups as to whether or not they are really protecting rights, or by following a specific ideology, perhaps are attempting to create "new" rights. Or are simply in many cases, looking at the strict letter of the law, as opposed to what the law actually intends.

"Rights" come with a measure of responsibility and respect for the public order, all of which must be taken into consideration.

Overall, the American experience has been one of exemplary conduct in regards to the protection of individual rights. Where there has been a lag in its practice, notably the refusal to grant full and equal rights to blacks, the very fact of their enslavement, and the second class status of women for much of American history, negates the good that the country has done in other areas. With the exception of the American Civil War, the country has proved itself to be more or less resilient in being able, for the most part, peacefully, to change when it has not lived up to its' stated ideals in practice. What has been called "the virtual bloodless civil rights revolution" is a case in point.

Though much effort and suffering accompanied the struggle for civil rights, in the end it did succeed in spite of all. The foundation of society was actually changed in such a profound way that would have been unheard of in many other countries. The strong tradition of freedom and liberty that was and is the underlying feature of American society allows our country to be a leader in civil rights.

How best to move forward with ensuring civil liberties and civil rights for all continues to dominate the national debate. In recent times, issues seem to revolve not around individual rights, but what has been called "group rights" has been raised. At the forefront of the debate is whether some specific remedies like affirmative action, quotas, gerrymandering and various other forms of preferential treatment are actually fair or just as bad as the ills they are supposed to cure. At the present no easy answers seem to be forthcoming. It is a testament to the American system that it has shown itself able to enter into these debates, to find solutions and tended to come out stronger.

The fact that the United States has the longest single constitutional history in the modern era is just one reason to be optimistic about the future of American liberty.

COMPETENCY 4.0   KNOWLEDGE OF ECONOMICS

Skill 4.1   **Analyze the effects of scarcity on the choices made by governments and individuals.**

Consumer economics is a focus within microeconomics which concentrates on the behavior of consumers. A **consumer** is a person who uses goods and services and, in a **capitalist** or free enterprise economy, decides with other consumers what is produced by what they choose to buy. **Consumers** are individuals or households that consume goods and services generated within the economy. Since this includes just about everyone, the term is a political term as much as an economic term when it is used in everyday speech. Typically when businesspeople and economists talk of *consumers* they are talking about *person as consumer*, an aggregated commodity item with little individuality other than that expressed in the buy/not-buy decision. A **consumer** is a person who buys and uses goods and services and, in a **capitalist** or free enterprise economy, decides with other consumers what is produced by what they choose to buy.

Capitalism is a social system based on the principle of individual rights. The term capitalism is used here in the broader philosophical political sense, and in the narrower economic sense, i.e. a free-market. In a free market, the term "supply and demand" is used to explain the influence of consumers on production. This law or principle of supply and demand means that prices of goods rise due to an increased demand and fall when there is an increase in the supply of goods.

In a free-enterprise economy, with individuals and groups determining what to buy or not buy there are fluctuations in the market brought about by oversupply or undersupply of goods consumers want to buy. This makes free enterprise economies inherently unstable. Due to unstable economies, inflation, job insecurity due to downsizing, bankruptcy and other factors, having cash on hand while buying is less prevalent than having **credit cards.** These cards are frequently referred to as "plastic money" but in reality are not money. They are a convenient tool for receiving a short-term loan from the financial institutions issuing the cards. Credit cards aid consumers in such economic activities as purchasing items on "installment plans." Financial institutions are not the only ones issuing credit cards. Oil companies, airlines, national automobile manufacturers, and large corporations are just some of the backers of credit cards. Credit card companies charge interest to the consumer on outstanding credit balances.

Department store charge cards do not enable the holder to obtain money from an **Automated Teller Machine (ATM)** but do enable one to buy on credit or on the installment plan. Automobile dealerships, banks, credit unions, loan companies all, in similar ways, make it possible for just about anyone to purchase on installment and drive a car. Mortgages allow people to pay for their own homes or condominiums.

Skill 4.2   Compare and contrast the characteristics of various economic systems.

Earlier forms of economic systems were based on barter or trade for goods and services. Current systems evolved out of the feudalism approach of the medieval Europe. Feudalism was based on land and agricultural development and ownership of land by the ruling class. Peasants worked the land and paid owners for the use of land through produce. Feudalism is viewed as the system which gave birth to modern economic systems. Those other important modern economic and ideological systems that have had the greatest effect in modern era are, *Socialism, Communism,* and *Fascism.*

Socialism – This is a fairly recent political phenomenon though its roots can be traced pretty far back in time in many respects. At the core, both socialism and communism are fundamentally economic philosophies that advocate public rather than private ownership, especially over means of production, yet even here, there are many distinctions. Karl Marx basically concentrated his attention on the industrial worker and on state domination over the means of production.

In practice, this Marxian dogma has largely been followed the most in those countries that profess to be Communist. In conjunction with massive programs for the development of heavy industry, this emphasis on production regardless of the wants or comforts of the individual in the given society. Socialism by contrast, usually occurring where industry has already been developed, has concerned itself more with the welfare of the individual and the fair distribution of whatever wealth is available.

Communism has a rigid theology, and a bible (*Das Capital*), that sees Communism emerging as a result of historic laws. Modern socialism is much closer to the ground. It too sees change in human society and hopes for improvement, but there is no unchanging millennium at the end of the road. Communism is sure that it will achieve the perfect state and in this certainty it is willing to use any and all means, however ruthless, to bring it about. Socialism on the other hand, confident only that the human condition is always changing, makes no easy approximation between ends and means and so cannot justify brutalities. This distinction in philosophy, of course, makes for an immense conflict in methods. Communism, believing that revolution is inevitable, works toward it by emphasizing class antagonisms. Socialism, while seeking change, insists on the use of democratic procedures within the existing social order of a given society. In it, the upper classes and capitalists are not to be violently overthrown but instead to be won over by logical persuasion.

It is interesting to note that in every perfect, idealized community or society that people have dreamed about throughout history, where human beings are pictured living in a special harmony that transcends their natural instincts, there has been a touch of socialism. This tendency was especially found in the *Utopian-Socialists* of the early 19th century, whose basic aim was the repudiation of the private-property system with its economic inefficiency and social injustice. Their criticisms rather than any actual achievements would linger after them. Like Marx, they envisioned industrial capitalism as becoming more and more inhumane and oppressive. They could not imagine the mass of workers prospering in such a system. Yet the workers soon developed their own powerful organizations and institutions. They began to bend the economic system to their own benefit. Thus a split did occur.

First, between those who after the growing success of the labor movement rejected the earlier utopian ideas as being impractical. Second, those who saw in this newfound political awareness of the working class a the key to organizing a societal revolution, saw this as inevitable based on their previous observations and study of history. Having reached a point where it has managed to jeopardize its very own survival, the inevitable revolution of those opposed to the capitalist system had to occur, history has proven this so, and history is always right and irrefutable. These believers in the absolute correctness of this doctrine gathered around Marx in what he called *Scientific Socialism*. In contempt to all other kinds which he considered not to be scientific, and therefore, useless as a realistic political philosophy.

The next split would occur between those who believed in the absolute inevitability of the coming revolution (the *Revolutionary Socialists* or as they came to be known, the *Communists*), and those while accepting the basic idea that the current capitalist system could not last, saw in the growing political awareness of the working class the beginnings of an ability to effect peaceful and gradual change in the social order. They believed this is better in the long run for everyone concerned as opposed to a cataclysmic, apocalyptic uprising (the *Democratic-Socialists*).

Major strides for the *Democratic-Socialists* were made before the First World War. A war that the Socialists, by philosophy pacifists, initially resisted, giving only reluctant support only once the struggle had begun. During the conflict, public sentiment against pacifism tended generally to weaken the movement, but with peace, reaction set in. The cause of world socialism leaped forward, often overcompensating by adhering to revolutionary communism which in the Revolution of 1917 had taken hold of in Russia. The between wars period saw the sudden spurt of socialism, whether their leanings were democratic or not, all socialists were bound together for a time in their resistance to fascism.

The decade following World War II saw tremendous growth in socialism. Economic planning and the nationalization of industry was undertaken in many countries and to this day have not been repudiated, though a subsequent return to self-confidence in the private business community and among voters, in general, has frequently weakened the socialist majority or reduced it to the status of an opposition party. This political balance leaves most industrialized countries with a mixed socialist-capitalist economy. So long as there is no major world-wide depression, this situation may remain relatively stable. The consequences of World War II, particularly the independence of former European colonies, has opened vast new areas for the attempted development of socialist forms. Most have tried to aspire to the democratic type but very few have succeeded except where democratic traditions were strong.

Socialism though concentrating on economic relationships, proposes a complete approach to human society. In effect, a new belief system and thus a world rather than a national movement. In this respect as well, it owes much to Great Britain for it was in London in 1864 that the first *Socialist International* was organized by Karl Marx. This radical leftist organization died off after limping along for twelve years, by which time its headquarters had moved to New York.

In 1889, the *Second Socialist International* met in Paris to celebrate the anniversary of the fall of the Bastille in the French Revolution. By this time, serious factions were developing. There were the **Anarchists**, who wanted to tear down everything, **Communists** who wanted to tear down the established order and build another in its place, and the **Democratic-Socialist** majority who favored peaceful political action.

Struggling for internal peace and cohesion right up to the First World War, socialism would remain largely ineffectual at this critical international time. Peace brought them all together again in Bern, Switzerland, but by this time the Soviet Union had been created, and the Russian Communists refused to attend the meeting on the ground that the Second Socialist International opposed the type of dictatorship it saw as necessary in order to achieve revolutions. Thus the *Communist International* was created in direct opposition to the Socialist International. While the socialists went on to advocate the "triumph of democracy, firmly rooted in the principles of liberty". The main objective of this new Socialist International was to maintain the peace, an ironic and very elusive goal in the period between the two world wars.

The Nazi attack on Poland in September, 1939, completely shattered the organization. In 1946, however a new *Socialist Information and Liaison Office* was set up to reestablish old contacts, and in 1951 the Communist International was revived with a conference in Frankfurt, Germany. At which time, it adopted a document entitled "Aims and Tasks of Democratic Socialism". A summary of these objectives gives a good picture of modern Democratic-Socialism as it exists on paper in its ideal form.

The first principle is the nationalized ownership of the major means of production and distribution. Usually public ownership is deemed appropriate for the strategically important services, public utilities, banking and resource industries such as coal, iron, lumber and oil. Farming has never been considered well adapted to public administration and has usually been excluded from nationalization. From this takeover of the free enterprise system, socialists expect a more perfect freedom to evolve. Offering equal opportunity for all, the minimizing of class conflict, better products for less cost, and security from physical want or need.

At the international level, socialism seeks a world of free peoples living together in peace and harmony for the mutual benefit of all. That freedom, at least from colonial rule, has largely been won. Peace throughout the world, however, is still as far off in most respects as it has ever been. According to the socialist doctrine, putting an end to capitalism will do much to reduce the likelihood of war. Armies and business are seen to need each other in a marriage of the weapons-mentality and devotion to private profit through the economic exploitation of weaker countries.

The United States remains the bastion of the free enterprise system. Socialism in the United States has long been regarded historically as a "menace" to the "American way". There is no question that socialists do argue for change. Capitalism in their opinion makes for unfair distribution of wealth, causing private affluence and public squalor. They also hold it responsible for environmental pollution and economic inflation. By curbing the absolute freedom of the private businessman or corporation, socialism hopes to satisfy all human necessities at the price of individual self-indulgence. Anti-trust legislation, the graduated income tax, and Social Security have all moved the United States toward the idea of the "welfare state", which recognizes as its prime objective full employment and a minimum living standard for all, whether employed or not. Even such taken for granted features of modern life as public schools and the federal postal service are relatively recent and socialistic innovations. Socialists applaud these programs, but, in what they regard as a sick society, these remedies seem to them only so much aspirin where major surgery is needed.

While communism and socialism arose in reaction to the excesses of 19th century capitalism, all three have matured in the past 100 years. Capitalism has mellowed, while a sibling rivalry may continue to exist between communism and socialism. Officially, communism clings to the idea of revolution and the seizing of capitalist property by the state without compensation, socialism accepts gradualism, feeling that a revolution, particularly in an industrial society would be ruinous. In fact, socialists and in some situations even communists, have come to realize that not all economic institutions function better in public hands. Private responsibility frequently offers benefits that go to the public good. This is particularly true in the agricultural sector, where personal ownership and cultivation of land have always been deeply ingrained.

All socialism denies certain freedoms, sometimes hidden in what it considers favorable terms. It deprives the minority of special economic privileges for the benefit of majority. The more left-wing, communistic socialism may deny the democratic process entirely. Traditionally defined, democracy holds to the idea that the people, exercising their majority opinion at the polls, will arrive at the common good by electing representative individuals to govern them. Communists would interpret this to mean the tyranny of an uneducated majority obliged to decide between a politically selected group of would-be leaders.

There is no question that the democratic process has its limitations, but for want of a better method, contemporary socialism accepts democracy as a major principle. Nowhere today does socialism exist in a pure and unchallenged form, but in many nations it has made impressive gains.

Communism – Is a direct outgrowth of socialism. In 1848, Karl Marx (with Freidrich Engels) began his **Communist Manifesto** with the prophetic sentence *"a specter is haunting Europe, the specter of communism"*. Little more than a century later, nearly one third of the world's population would live under governments professing communism. Even with the collapse of the Soviet Union and the Eastern Communist Block, China with nearly one fourth of the world's population, not to mention North Korea and Cuba, still claim to follow the communist ideal. Yet, in these societies, not one of them could say that they have achieved, (through massive toil, treachery and bloodshed), the ideal state that communism was supposed to create.

Marx took the name for his ideal society from the *French Communes*, feudal villages that held land and produce in common. But he was not satisfied with villages. His dream was of newly industrialized Europe shaped into a communist world. As he saw it, other systems would give way, or if they fought back, would be destroyed. With the birth of the industrial age in the early 19th century, privately owned factories employed larger and larger work forces. The owners of these factories made vast profits, which they plowed back into building more factories. The workers were becoming mere tools in a huge anonymous crowd, alienated from the product of their toil. Labor was hard, often dangerous, and poorly rewarded.

Marx saw capitalism in its formative years as leading only to increased enrichment of the owners of great businesses and to the eventual enslavement of the working class. Marx exhorted the workers to revolt. He urged them in his writings to seize the factories from the capitalists, not in order to become capitalist themselves, but in order to place the means of production in the hands of the community for the benefit of all its citizens. This intermediate society controlling the means of production is called the *"Dictatorship of the Proletariat"*. It is what the Soviet Union and other so-called communist nations achieved, but it is not communism. True communism comes only with the further step of the state giving ownership back to the people, who then continue to live together in abundance without supervision from a ruling class.

Pure Communism does not now, (in those few countries that still profess it), nor has it ever, existed in actual fact. So, despite endless writing on the subject of communism, almost all of its verbiage has been devoted to the struggle to achieve socialism. Today for the commissar who drives the worker, and the peasant who pulls the load, communism still remains the goal, the end of the struggle. Though Marx and his disciples have insisted and continue to insist that socialism is only a stop on the way to communism, they have not dared to describe this final paradise on Earth except in the haziest of ways.

With the final achievement of communism, greed and competition will presumably cease. Each person will contribute according to their ability and receive according to their need. There will be no cause for crime or vice of any kind. No race or class rivalry, no grounds for war, and no reason for government.
In fact, it is not measurably nearer today anywhere than when Marx first conceived it.

Fascism – The last important historical economic system to arise. It has been called a reaction against the last two ideologies discussed. It can, at times, cooperate with a Monarchy if it has to.

In general, Fascism is the effort to create, by dictatorial means, a viable national society in which competing interests were to be adjusted to each other by being entirely subordinated to the service of the state. The following features have been characteristic of Fascism in its various manifestations: **(1)** An origin at a time of serious economic disruption and of rapid and bewildering social change. **(2)** A philosophy that rejects democratic and humanitarian ideals and glorifies the absolute sovereignty of the state, the unity and destiny of the people, and their unquestioning loyalty and obedience to the dictator. **(3)** An aggressive nationalism which calls for the mobilization and regimentation of every aspect of national life and makes open use of violence and intimidation. **(4)** The simulation of mass popular support, accomplished by outlawing all but a single political party and by using suppression, censorship, and propaganda. **(5)** A program of vigorous action including economic reconstruction, industrialization, pursuit of economic self-sufficiency, territorial expansion and war which is dramatized as bold, adventurous, and promising a glorious future.

Fascist movements often had socialists origins. For example, in Italy, where fascism first arose in place of socialism, **Benito Mussolini**, sought to impose what he called "*corporativism*". A fascist "*corporate*" state would, in theory, run the economy for the benefit of the whole country like a corporation. It would be centrally controlled and managed by an elite who would see that its benefits would go to everyone.

Fascism has always declared itself the uncompromising enemy of communism, with which, however, fascist actions have much in common. (In fact, many of the methods of organization and propaganda used by fascists were taken from the experience of the early Russian communists, along with the belief in a single strong political party, secret police, etc.) The propertied interests and the upper classes, fearful of revolution, often gave their support to fascism on the basis of promises by the fascist leaders to maintain the status quo and safeguard property. (In effect, accomplishing a revolution from above with their help as opposed from below against them. However, fascism did consider itself a revolutionary movement of a different type).

Once established, a fascist regime ruthlessly crushes communist and socialist parties as well as all democratic opposition. It regiments the propertied interests to its national goals and wins the potentially revolutionary masses to fascist programs by substituting a rabid nationalism for class conflict. Thus fascism may be regarded as an extreme defensive expedient adopted by a nation faced with the sometimes illusionary threat of communist subversion or revolution. Under fascism, capital is regulated as much as labor and fascist contempt for legal or constitutional guarantees effectively destroyed whatever security the capitalistic system had enjoyed under pre-fascist governments.

In addition, fascist or similar regimes are at times anti-Communist. This is evidenced by the Soviet-German treaty of 1939. During the period of alliance created by the treaty, Italy and Germany and their satellite countries ceased their anti-Communist propaganda. They emphasized their own revolutionary and proletarian origins and attacked the so-called plutocratic western democracies.

The fact that fascist countries sought to control national life by methods identical to those of communist governments make such nations vulnerable to communism after the fascist regime is destroyed.

In theory at least, the chief distinction between fascism and communism is that fascism is *nationalist*, exalting the interests of the state and glorifying war between nations, whereas, communism is *internationalist*, exalting the interests of a specific economic class (the proletariat) and glorifying world wide class warfare. In practice, however, this fundamental distinction loses some of its validity. For in its heyday, fascism was also an internationalist movement. A movement dedicated to world conquest, (like communism), as evidenced by the events prior to and during the Second World War. At the same time, many elements in communism as it evolved came to be very nationalistic as well.

Skill 4.3 Identify the role of markets in decisions affecting production, distribution, and consumption.

A "market" is an economic term to describe the places and situations in which goods and services are bought and sold. In a capitalistic free enterprise economy, the market prices of goods and services rise and fall according to decreases and increases in the supply and demand and the degree of competition.

In an economic system, there is also a "market" for land, capital, and labor. The labor market, for example, is studied by economists in order to better understand trends in jobs, productivity of workers, activities of labor unions, and patterns of employment. Potential customers for a product or service are called a **market** and are the subject of **market research** to determine who would possibly make use of whatever is offered to customers.

Other types of markets, which are part of countries' economic systems, include the following:

Stock Market
This is part of a capitalistic free enterprise system and is one of significant investment and speculation. Any changes in the prices of stocks are seriously affected by those who buy stocks when their prices are rising and sell them when their prices are falling. Business planners quite often regard the stock market as a barometer of the degree of confidence investors have in the conditions of businesses in the future. When the stock market is a rising "bull" market, economists and investors see it as the public showing confidence in the future of business. At the same time, when the market is a falling "bear" market, it is an indication of a lack of confidence. In unstable economic conditions, one or more conditions and situations can seriously affect the stock market's rise and fall. The "bottom line" is that these fluctuations are directly tied to and directly affected by investment changes.

"Black" Market
This illegal market has in the past and even today exists in countries where wage and price controls are in place and enforced by law. In these markets, goods and products are priced and sold above legal limits, especially if the maximum legal price is much less than free-market price. The black market thrives when certain products are unavailable in the regulated market and there is a demand for them, or if wage and price controls are in place for an extended period.

Common Market
This market, also known as the European Economic Community (EEC), began in 1958 and is comprised of several European nations. Its major purpose was to remove all restrictive tariffs and import quotas in order to encourage and facilitate free trade among member nations. Included were efforts to move workers and services without restrictions.

Skill 4.4   Evaluate factors to consider when making consumer decisions.

Economics is divided into two broad categories: *macroeconomics* and *microeconomics*. Macroeconomics is a study of the aggregates that comprise the economy on the national level: output, consumption, investment, government spending, and net exports. Microeconomics is a study of the economy at the industry or firm level. Microeconomics is concerned with consumer behavior, output and input markets, and the distribution of income.

A firm's production decisions are based on its costs. Every product is produced using inputs or resources. These are called *factors of production*, and there are four that are used in the production of every good and service: labor, land, capital, and entrepreneurship. The firm hires these factors in the input or resource market. The production process refers to the method in which resources are combined to produce a good or service. The costs for *fixed factors* of production, such as land, plant, and equipment, are called fixed costs. The costs for *variable factors*, such as labor, are called variable costs. Costs of production, then, are the total of fixed and variable costs.

Each factor of production earns its factor income in the resource market. Labor earns wages, capital earns interest, land earns rent, and the entrepreneur earns profit. The size of the factor income depends on the scarcity of the factor and the significance of its contribution to the production process. A market economy does not result in the equality of income. Each factor earns an income based on its contribution.

Firms sell their outputs in different output market structures. There are four kinds of market structures in the output market: perfect competition, monopoly, monopolistic competition, and oligopoly.

For the most part, perfect competition is a theoretical extreme, most closely approximated by agriculture. The numerous firms sell a product identical to that sold by all other firms in the industry and have no control over the price. The price is a given to the firm. Buyers and sellers have full market information, and there are no barriers to entry. A barrier to entry is anything that makes it difficult for firms to enter or leave the industry.

The opposite of a perfectly competitive firm is a monopolist. Monopoly is a market structure in which there is only one seller who can control his price. The firm is equal to the industry. A monopolist becomes a monopolist and remains a monopolist because of barriers to entry, which are very high. These barriers to entry include a very high fixed cost structure, which functions to keep new firms from entering the industry. Monopoly is illegal in the U.S. economy.

Between the two extremes are the two market structures that all U.S. firms fall into. Oligopoly is a market structure in which there are a few sellers of products that may be either homogeneous (steel), or heterogeneous (automobiles). There are high barriers to entry, which is why there are only a few firms in each industry.

Monopolistic competition is the situation you see in shopping centers. There are numerous firms, each selling products that are similar but not identical, such as brand name shoes or clothing. Barriers to entry are not as high as in an oligopoly which is why there are more firms.

Demand is based on consumer preferences. Satisfaction refers to the quantities of a good or service that buyers are willing and able to buy at different prices during a given period of time. Supply is based on costs of production and refers to the quantities that sellers are willing and able to sell at different prices during a given period of time. The determination of market equilibrium price is when the decisions of buyers coincide with the decisions of sellers.

Demand curves and supply curves have different shapes. We can define the term *elasticity* to be a measure of the responsiveness of quantity to changes in price. If quantity is very responsive to changes in price, then demand is said to be elastic; if quantity is not very responsive to changes in price, then demand is inelastic.

Skill 4.5   Identify the advantages and disadvantages of various kinds of credit.

The part of an economy that is centered on the consumer rather than the economy between businesses is called a consumer economy. This is the part of an economy where services and finished goods are purchased by individuals for their own use. The purchase of clothing, automobiles, telephone service, personal computers, or CDs are all part of the consumer economy.

This is a crucial part of most economies, and credit plays an important role in driving it. Credit is simply a promise to pay for goods or services that have already been provided. Credit lenders such as credit card companies and banks allow borrowers to pay back these loans over time. For this service, they charge fees and interest on the balance of the loan. The money made from fees and interest finance, in part, the extension of credit to more people.

Some consumer purchases, such as automobiles and homes, are so expensive that most people would have to save for many years to buy one for cash. Credit allows consumers to pay a small portion of the total cost up front and borrow the balance. Without credit, these purchases would simply be impossible for many people. With credit, a market exists for a steady stream of new houses and cars "Globalism" is defined as the principle of the interdependence of all the world's nations and their peoples. Within this global community, every nation, to a certain degree, is dependent on other nations. Since no one nation has all of the resources needed for production, trade with other nations is required to obtain what is needed for production, to sell what is produced or to buy finished products, to earn money to maintain and strengthen the nation's economic system.

Developing nations receive technical assistance and financial aid from developed nations. Many international organizations have been created to promote and encourage cooperation and economic progress among member nations. In a Utopian society, all countries would be free to sell their resources and products at whatever price consumers were willing to buy them. However, countries and regions are unequally able to supply various goods. Climate and geography determine to some extent what countries can grow wheat, for example, and how far they will need to ship it to get it to the buyers. Thus, it is necessary for countries to cooperate in world markets to aid developing and industrialized nations to compete in global markets.

Trade is an important element in the global economic systems. Countries export goods and services to other countries and import goods and services into the country. The World Trade Organization was established by primarily free-market countries, to have some control of the buying and selling of goods on a global market. Another international organization is OPEC, created by the primary oil-producing nations in an effort to control the production and pricing of oil throughout the world. Through the setting up and elimination of such barriers to trade as tariffs, trade is stimulated resulting in increased productivity, economic progress, increased cooperation and understanding on diplomatic levels.

Those nations not part of an international trade organization not only must make those economic decisions of what to produce, how and for whom, but must also deal with the problem of tariffs and quotas on imports. Regardless of international trade memberships, economic growth and development are vital and affect all trading nations. Businesses, labor, and governments share common interests and goals in a nation's economic status. International systems of banking and finance have been devised to assist governments and businesses in setting the policy and guidelines for the exchange of currencies. "Globalism" is defined as the principle of the interdependence of all the world's nations and their peoples. Within this global community, every nation, to a certain degree, is dependent on other nations. Since no one nation has all of the resources needed for production, trade with other nations is required to obtain what is needed for production, to sell what is produced or to buy finished products, to earn money to maintain and strengthen the nation's economic system.

Developing nations receive technical assistance and financial aid from developed nations. Many international organizations have been created to promote and encourage cooperation and economic progress among member nations. In a Utopian society, all countries would be free to sell their resources and products at whatever price consumers were willing to buy them. However, countries and regions are unequally able to supply various goods. Climate and geography determine to some extent what countries can grow wheat, for example, and how far they will need to ship it to get it to the buyers. Thus, it is necessary for countries to cooperate in world markets to aid developing and industrialized nations to compete in global markets.

Trade is an important element in the global economic systems. Countries export goods and services to other countries and import goods and services into the country. The World Trade Organization was established by primarily free-market countries, to have some control of the buying and selling of goods on a global market. Another international organization is OPEC, created by the primary oil-producing nations in an effort to control the production and pricing of oil throughout the world. Through the setting up and elimination of such barriers to trade as tariffs, trade is stimulated resulting in increased productivity, economic progress, increased cooperation and understanding on diplomatic levels.

Those nations not part of an international trade organization not only must make those economic decisions of what to produce, how and for whom, but must also deal with the problem of tariffs and quotas on imports. Regardless of international trade memberships, economic growth and development are vital and affect all trading nations. Businesses, labor, and governments share common interests and goals in a nation's economic status. International systems of banking and finance have been devised to assist governments and businesses in setting the policy and guidelines for the exchange of currencies.

and supports construction and the auto industry. In addition, the financial services connected to the administration and collections of credit payments comprise an important part of the overall economy. Loans can be traded similar to other financial instruments such as stocks and bonds. The consumer economy is the foundation of a large portion of the overall economy.

Credit creates debt, which can have an economic downside. As can be seen, some debt is good for an economy, because it drives the services and industries tied to the consumer economy. Consumer debt becomes a problem, however, when it becomes so large that consumers cannot repay it. Some of this debt is insured by the government, such as certain home loans in the U.S., and when borrowers default, public funds are used to pay the lender. In some cases, individuals who cannot pay their debts seek legal protection by claiming bankruptcy. In these cases, the companies that provided the goods and services to that individual may never be paid, creating a loss.

Skill 4.6   Identify the factors involved in global economic interdependence and trade between nations.

"Globalism" is defined as the principle of the interdependence of all the world's nations and their peoples. Within this global community, every nation, to a certain degree, is dependent on other nations. Since no one nation has all of the resources needed for production, trade with other nations is required to obtain what is needed for production, to sell what is produced or to buy finished products, to earn money to maintain and strengthen the nation's economic system.

Developing nations receive technical assistance and financial aid from developed nations. Many international organizations have been created to promote and encourage cooperation and economic progress among member nations. In a Utopian society, all countries would be free to sell their resources and products at whatever price consumers were willing to buy them. However, countries and regions are unequally able to supply various goods. Climate and geography determine to some extent what countries can grow wheat, for example, and how far they will need to ship it to get it to the buyers. Thus, it is necessary for countries to cooperate in world markets to aid developing and industrialized nations to compete in global markets.

Trade is an important element in the global economic systems. Countries export goods and services to other countries and import goods and services into the country. The World Trade Organization was established by primarily free-market countries, to have some control of the buying and selling of goods on a global market. Another international organization is OPEC, created by the primary oil-producing nations in an effort to control the production and pricing of oil throughout the world. Through the setting up and elimination of such barriers to trade as tariffs, trade is stimulated resulting in increased productivity, economic progress, increased cooperation and understanding on diplomatic levels.

Those nations not part of an international trade organization not only must make those economic decisions of what to produce, how and for whom, but must also deal with the problem of tariffs and quotas on imports. Regardless of international trade memberships, economic growth and development are vital and affect all trading nations. Businesses, labor, and governments share common interests and goals in a nation's economic status. International systems of banking and finance have been devised to assist governments and businesses in setting the policy and guidelines for the exchange of currencies.

Skill 4.7   Identify the purposes and effects of various types of taxes.

Taxes are enforced contributions which citizens make in order to fund government. These monies go to fund public safety, education, sanitation, transportation and various welfare programs. In order to pay for the functions of government, taxes are levied at the federal, state, and local level. The politics of taxes differ from region to region and from the local to federal level.

Income Tax

Most income taxes are progressive. Thus the more money you make, the higher tax rate you will pay. Direct withholding, a process in which an employer automatically deducts taxes, is the most common way people pay income tax.

Retirement Tax

Over a lifetime, worker's contribute to social security. In this system money is taken out of each paycheck to fund the social security system. Once eligible, a citizen will be able to withdraw a certain amount from the system each month.

Capital Gains Tax

When an investment is cashed out and profit is made, the profit is taxed. Thus a portion of any profit made must be paid in taxes.

Excise Tax

This is a common tax placed on purchased items. An excise tax takes into account the quantity of the purchased item. Examples of excise taxes include gasoline taxes and sales tax.

Tariff

A tariff is a tax for moving goods across a political border. If a foreign country produces a product very cheaply, a tariff can be imposed thus making that product less profitable. Tariffs are often used to protect domestic industry.

Property Tax

Property taxes are paid based on the value of land owned. These types of taxes are used to fund local and state services. In many states public safety is heavily funded by property taxes.

COMPETENCY 5.0   KNOWLEDGE OF SOCIAL SCIENCE CURRICULUM AND INSTRUCTION

Skill 5.1   **Identify the interdisciplinary relationships of the social sciences.**

The major disciplines within the social sciences are definitely intertwined and interrelated. Knowledge and expertise in one requires background that involves some or most of the others.

Anthropology is the field of study of human culture--how different groups of people live, how they have adapted to their physical environment, what they make or produce, and their relationship to other cultures, behavior, differences and similarities. To pursue the study of people, the anthropologist must know the history of the people being studied; their geography--physical environment; their governmental structure, organization, and its impact on the people; sociology is closely related to this field so knowledge and study in this area is helpful; their goods and produce and how they are used tie in with a background of economics.

Archaeology studies human cultures in the past, examining artifacts left behind to determine how certain people or groups lived their daily lives. Certainly, knowledge of history gives a background as a foundation of study. Geography makes its contribution by not only knowing where to look for remains but also how geographic conditions contributed to and affected the people or cultural groups being studied; how physical factors contributed to artifacts left behind.

Civics deals with what is required and expected of a region's citizens, their rights and responsibilities to government and each other. Knowledge of history gives the background and foundation and government or political science explains not only the organization and set-up of the government but also the impact of international relations on the country or area.

Economics also involves the study of history, geography, and political science. The different interrelationships include. History is used to examine economic theory and principles and to understand the historical background of areas. The economic activities in different countries, regions of the world and how international trade and relations are affected also leads to political science or how political systems impact economies...

Geography is the study of the earth, its people, and how people adapt to life on earth and how they use its resources. It is undeniably connected to history, economics, political science, sociology, anthropology, and even a bit of archaeology. Geography not only deals with people and the earth today but also with historic and cultural behavior: evolution of economies of a region and the comparative advantage of geographic location; how people interact with the physical environment. Geography can play a role in all of the social science disciplines.

History is without doubt an integral part of every other discipline in the social sciences. Knowing historical background helps to explain geographic, political, economic, psychological, sociological and cultural behavior and patterns.

Political Science is the study of government, international relations, political thought and activity, and comparison of governments. It is tied in with history (historical background), anthropology (how government affects a group's culture and relationship with other groups), economics (governmental influence and regulation of producing and distributing goods and products), and sociology (insight into how social developments affect political life). Other disciplines are also affected, as the study of political science is crucial to understanding the political processes and the influence of government, civic duties, and responsibilities of people.

Psychology is defined as scientifically studying mental processes and behavior. It is related to anthropology and sociology, two social sciences that also study people in society. All three closely consider relationships and attitudes of humans within their social settings. Anthropology considers humans within their cultures, how they live, what they make or produce, how different groups or cultures relate to each other. Sociology follows the angle of looking at behaviors, attitudes, conditions, and relationships in human society. Psychology focuses on individual behavior and how actions are influenced by feelings and beliefs. Individual behavior effects political, economic and sociological behavior, as well.

Sociology studies human society with its attitudes, behaviors, conditions, and relationships with others. It is closely related to anthropology, especially applied to groups outside of one's region, nation, or hemisphere. History puts it in perspective with an historical background. Political Science is tied to sociology with the impact of political and governmental regulation of activities. Awareness of, influence of, and use of the physical environment as studied in geography also contributes to understanding. Economic activities are a part of human society. The field of psychology is also related.

Skill 5.2   **Apply nontextbook resources (e.g., technology, media, community) for use in social science instruction).**

The interdisciplinary curriculum planning approach to student learning creates a meaningful balance inclusive of curriculum depth and breadth. Take for instance the following scenario: Mrs. Jackson presents her 9A Language Arts class with an assignment for collaborative group work. She provides them with the birth date and death of the infamous author Ernest Hemingway and asks them to figure how old he was when he died. She gives them five minutes as a group to work on the final answer. After five minutes, she asks each group for their answer and writes the answers on the board. Each group gives a different answer. When Mrs. Jackson comes to the last group, a female student states, "Why do we have to do math in a Language Arts class?"

The application of knowledge learned from a basic math class would have problem-solved the Language Arts' question. Given the date of his birth and the date of his death, all students needed to do was subtract his birth from his death year to come up with a numerical answer = age when he died. Providing students with a constructivist modality of applying knowledge to problem-solve pertinent information for a language arts' class should be an integral part of instructional practice and learning in an interdisciplinary classroom.

Historically, previous centuries of educational research have shown a strong correlation between the need for interdisciplinary instruction and cognitive learning application. Understanding how students process information and create learning was the goal of earlier educators. Earlier researchers looked at how the brain connected information pieces into meaning and found that learning takes place along intricate neural pathways that formulate processing and meaning from data input into the brain. The implications for student learning are vast in that teachers can work with students to break down subject content area into bits of information that can be memorized and applied to a former learning experience and then processed into integral resources of information.

Technology

The Internet and other research resources provide a wealth of information on thousands of interesting topics for students preparing presentations or projects. Using search engines like Google, Microsoft and Infotrac allow students to search multiple Internet resources or databases on one subject search. Students should have an outline of the purpose of a project or research presentation that includes:

- Purpose - identity the reason for the research information
- Objective - having a clear thesis for a project will allow the students opportunities to be specific on Internet searches
- Preparation - when using resources or collecting data, students should create folders for sorting through the information. Providing labels for the folders will create a system of organization that will make construction of the final project or presentation easier and less time consuming
- Procedure - organized folders and a procedural list of what the project or presentation needs to include will create A+ work for students and A+ grading for teachers
- Visuals or artifacts - choose data or visuals that are specific to the subject content or presentation. Make sure that poster boards or PowerPoint presentations can be visually seen from all areas of the classroom. Teachers can provide laptop computers for PowerPoint presentations.

Having the school's librarian or technology expert as a guest speaker in classrooms provides another method of sharing and modeling proper presentation preparation using technology. Teachers can also appoint technology experts from the students in a classroom to work with students on projects and presentations. In high schools, technology classes provide students with upper-class teacher assistants who fill the role of technology assistants.

Skill 5.3 **Identify how social science content can be integrated with other areas of the curriculum.**

See Skill 5.2

Skill 5.4 **Identify various assessment strategies for the social sciences.**

In order to provide students with the broadest education possible it is important to provide them with a variety of assessments.

Beyond multiple-choice tests, essays, constructed responses, and projects social studies educators are continually formulating new assessment strategies. The discipline of social studies is a perfect area to be creative and use cutting edge assessments in order to accurately gauge the progress of students in such a broad arena.

Skill 5.5 **Select strategies for teaching the social sciences to differentiated populations.**

Social studies as a discipline is one of the best subject areas to effectively differentiate instruction. Project based learning also offers a great opportunity to tailor assignments to student's abilities.

Tips to help differentiate

1) Move through material sequentially
2) Include visual aides during lectures
3) Emphasize key concepts in each period
4) Use a variety of instructional aides including text and video
5) Compare and contrast the present with the past
6) Include multiple points of view
7) Offer multiple choices for projects
8) Allow students multiple assessment options

Skill 5.6 **Identify strategies for teaching the use of social science resources (e.g., primary source documents, charts, maps, graphs).**

See Skill 5.2

Bibliography

Adams, James Truslow. (2006). "The March of Democracy," Vol 1. "The Rise of the Union". New York: Charles Scribner's Sons, Publisher.

Barbini, John & Warshaw, Steven. (2006). "The World Past and Present." New York: Harcourt, Brace, Jovanovich, Publishers.

Berthon, Simon & Robinson, Andrew. (2006. "The Shape of the World." Chicago: Rand McNally, Publisher.

Bice, David A. (2006). "A Panorama of Florida II". (Second Edition). Marceline, Missouri: Walsworth Publishing Co., Inc.

Bram, Leon (Vice-President and Editorial Director). (2006). "Funk and Wagnalls New Encyclopedia." United States of America.

Burns, Edward McNall & Ralph, Philip Lee. (2006. "World Civilizations Their History and Culture" (5th ed.). New York: W.W. Norton & Company, Inc., Publishers.

Dauben, Joseph W. (2006). "The World Book Encyclopedia." Chicago: World Book Inc. A Scott Fetzer Company, Publisher.

De Blij, H.J. & Muller, Peter O. (2006). "Geography Regions and Concepts" (Sixth Edition). New York: John Wiley & Sons, Inc., Publisher.

Encyclopedia Americana. (2006). Danbury, Connecticut: Grolier Incorporated, Publisher.

Heigh, Christopher (Editor). (2006). "The Cambridge Historical Encyclopedia of Great Britain and Ireland." Cambridge: Cambridge University Press, Publisher.

Hunkins, Francis P. & Armstrong, David G. (2006). "World Geography People and Places." Columbus, Ohio: Charles E. Merrill Publishing Co. A Bell & Howell Company, Publishers.

Jarolimek, John; Anderson, J. Hubert & Durand, Loyal, Jr. (2006). "World Neighbors." New York: Macmillan Publishing Company. London: Collier Macmillan Publishers.

McConnell, Campbell R. (2006). "Economics-Principles, Problems, and Policies" (Tenth Edition). New York: McGraw-Hill Book Company, Publisher.

Millard, Dr. Anne & Vanags, Patricia. (2006). "The Usborne Book of World History." London: Usborne Publishing Ltd., Publisher.

Novosad, Charles (Executive Editor). (2006). "The Nystrom Desk Atlas." Chicago: Nystrom Division of Herff Jones, Inc., Publisher.

Patton, Clyde P.; Rengert, Arlene C.; Saveland, Robert N.; Cooper, Kenneth S. & Cam, Patricia T. (2006). "A World View." Morristown, N.J.: Silver Burdette Companion, Publisher.

Schwartz, Melvin & O'Connor, John R. (2006). "Exploring A Changing World." New York: Globe Book Company, Publisher.
"The Annals of America: Selected Readings on Great Issues in American History 1620-1968." (2006). United States of America: William Benton, Publisher.

Tindall, George Brown & Shi, David E. (2006). "America-A Narrative History" (Fourth Edition). New York: W.W. Norton & Company, Publisher.
Todd, Lewis Paul & Curti, Merle. (2006). "Rise of the American Nation" (Third Edition). New York: Harcourt, Brace, Jovanovich, Inc., Publishers.

Tyler, Jenny; Watts, Lisa; Bowyer, Carol; Trundle, Roma & Warrender, Annabelle (2006) 'The Usbome Book of World Geography." London: Usbome Publishing Ltd., Publisher.

Willson, David H. (2006). "A History of England." Hinsdale, Illinois: The Dryder Press, Inc. Publisher.

Sample Test

1. The important issues in the 20h century were:
    (Skill 1.1) (Easy)

    A. Political

    B. Economic

    C. Historical

    D. Social

2. The Age of Exploration begun in the 1400s was led by:
    (Skill 1.1) (Average)

    A. The Portuguese

    B. The Spanish

    C. The English

    D. The Dutch

3. Bartholomeu Dias, in seeking a route around the tip of Africa, was forced to turn back. Nevertheless, the cape he discovered near the southern tip of Africa became known as:
    (Skill 1.1) (Rigorous)

    A. Cape Horn

    B. Cabo Bojador

    C. Cape of Good Hope

    D. Cape Hatteras

4. Which of the following developments is most closely associated with the Neolithic Age?
    (Skill 1.1) (Rigorous)

    A. Human use of fire

    B. First use of stone chipping instruments

    C. Domestication of animals

    D. Development of metallurgical alloys

5. Which does not apply to the ancient Assyrians?
    (Skill 1.1) (Rigorous)

    A. Developed maps

    B. Warlike

    C. Organized military

    D. Horse Drawn Chariots

6. Which of the following is not a religion of China:
    (Skill 1.3) (Average)

    A. Confucianism

    B. Taoism

    C. Buddhism

    D. Shintoism

7. The first ancient civilization to introduce and practice monotheism was the:
(Skill 1.3) (Average)

   A. Sumerians

   B. Hebrews

   C. Phoenicians

   D. Minoans

8. Which of the following is not a result of the Industrial Revolution?
(Skill 1.4) (Rigorous)

   A. Growth of cities

   B. Increased productivity

   C. Specialization and division of labor

   D. Rise in religious tolerance

9. The area of the United States was effectively doubled through purchase of the Louisiana Territory under which President?
(Skill 1.4) (Rigorous)

   A. John Adams

   B. Thomas Jefferson

   C. James Madison

   D. James Monroe

10. The politics of classical Athens is best described by which of the following?
(Skill 1.5) (Average)

   A. Limited democracy, including both slaves and free men

   B. One man dictatorial rule

   C. Universal democracy among free owners of property

   D. Oligarchy with a few families controlling all decisions

11. The Pax Romana resulted in all but the following:
(Skill 1.5) (Average)

   A. Free travel and trade

   B. The Punic Wars

   C. Expansion of Culture

   D. A long period of peace

12. Secularism was the most significant aspect of all but the following civilizations:
(Skill 1.5) (Rigorous)

   A. Greek

   B. Sumerian

   C. Hellenic

   D. Roman

13. The Compromise of 1850 came about as a result of which state's entry into the Union?
(Skill 1.5) (Average)

A. Texas

B. Missouri

C. California

D. Kansas

14. The last Czar of Russia was:
(Skill 1.6) (Average)

A. Peter the Great

B. Ivan the Terrible

C. Nicholas II

D. Catherine the Great

15. Chinese civilization is generally credited with the original development of which of the following sets of technologies:
(Skill 1.6) (Rigorous)

A. Movable type and mass production of goods

B. Wool processing and domestication of the horse

C. Paper and gunpowder manufacture

D. Leather processing and modern timekeeping

16. Which was not one of the five major tribes of the Middle Ages?
(Skill 1.6) (Rigorous)

A. Visigoths

B. Saxons

C. Vandals

D. Phoenicians

17. The painter of the Sistine Ceiling was:
(Skill 1.6) (Easy)

A. Raphael

B. Michelangelo

C. Leonardo da Vinci

D. Titian

18. Church abuses leading to the Protestant Revolution included all but:
(Skill 1.6) (Rigorous)

A. Disagreement over the role of Jesus Christ

B. Sale of dispensations

C. The sale of indulgences, whereby the buyer may purchase purgation of Sins

D. Fraudulent clergy

19. The Renaissance began in:
(Skill 1.6) (Average)

A. Florence

B. Greece

C. England

D. France

20. The first explorer to reach India by sailing around the southern tip of Africa was:
(Skill 1.6) (Average)

A. Amerigo Vespucci

B. Vasco da Gama

C. Ferdinand Magellan

D. John Cabot

21. Great Britain became the center of technological and industrial development during the nineteenth century chiefly on the basis of:
(Skill 1.6) (Rigorous)

A. Central location relative to the population centers of Europe

B. Colonial conquests and military victories over European powers

C. Reliance on exterior sources of financing

D. Resources of coal and production of steel

22. Which of the following is not associated with the Age of Exploration?
(Skill 1.6) (Rigorous)

A. The need for food

B. The Vivaldo Brothers

C. Marco Polo

D. The quest for trade routes

23. Which revolution occurred the latest:
(Skill 1.6) (Average)

A. American Revolution

B. French Revolution

C. Chinese Revolution

D. Russian Revolution

24. The belief that the United States should control all of North America was called:
(Skill 1.7) (Average)

A. Westward Expansion

B. Pan Americanism

C. Manifest Destiny

D. Nationalism

25. Of all the major causes of both World Wars I and II, the most significant one is considered to be:
(Skill 1.7) (Rigorous)

A. Extreme nationalism

B. Military buildup and aggression

C. Political unrest

D. Agreements and alliances

26. Leaders in the movement for woman's rights have included all but:
(Skill 1.7) (Rigorous)

A. Elizabeth Cady Stanton

B. Lucretia Borgia

C. Susan B. Anthony

D. Lucretia Mott

27. The Middle Colonies of the Americas were:
(Skill 1.7) (Average)

A. Maryland, Virginia, North Carolina

B. New York, New Jersey, Pennsylvania, Delaware

C. Rhode Island, Connecticut, New York, New Jersey

D. Vermont and New Hampshire

28. Slavery arose in the Southern Colonies partly as a perceived economical way to:
(Skill 1.7) (Average)

A. Increase the owner's wealth through human beings used as a source of exchange

B. Cultivate large plantations of cotton, tobacco, rice, indigo, and other crops

C. Provide Africans with humanitarian aid, such as health care, Christianity, and literacy

D. Keep ships' holds full of cargo on two out of three legs of the "triangular trade" voyage

29. France decided in 1777 to help the American colonies in their war against Britain. This decision was based on:
(Skill 1.7) (Rigorous)

A. The naval victory of John Paul Jones over the British ship Serapis"

B. The survival of the terrible winter at Valley Forge

C. The success of colonial guerilla fighters in the South

D. The defeat of the British at Saratoga

30. **A major quarrel between colonial Americans and the British concerned a series of British Acts of Parliament dealing with:**
(Skill 1.7) (Average)

   A. Taxes

   B. Slavery

   C. Native Americans

   D. Shipbuilding

31. **The first shots in what was to become the American Revolution were fired in:**
(Skill 1.7) (Average)

   A. Florida

   B. Massachusetts

   C. New York

   D. Virginia

32. **Of the following, which contributed most to penetration of western areas by colonial Americans?**
(Skill 1.7) (Rigorous)

   A. Development of large ships capable of sailing upstream in rivers such as the Hudson, Susquehanna, and Delaware

   B. The invention of the steamboat

   C. Improved relations with Native Americans, who invited colonial Americans to travel west to settle

   D. Improved roads, mail service, and communications

33. **What was a major source of contention between American settlers in Texas and the Mexican government in the 1830s and 1840s? (Skill 1.7) (Rigorous)**

A. The Americans wished to retain slavery, which had been outlawed in Mexico

B. The Americans had agreed to learn Spanish and become Roman Catholic, but failed to do so

C. The Americans retained ties to the United States, and Santa Ana feared the power of the U.S.

D. All of the above were contentious issues between American settlers and the Mexican government

34. **A consequence of the Gold Rush of Americans to California in 1848 and 1849 was that: (Skill 1.7) (Rigorous)**

A. California spent the minimum amount of time as a territory and was admitted as a slave state

B. California was denied admission on its first application, since most Americans felt that the settlers were too "uncivilized" to deserve statehood

C. California was purchased from Mexico for the express purpose of gaining immediate statehood

D. California did not go through the normal territorial stage but applied directly for statehood as a free state

35. **The principle of "popular sovereignty" allowing people in any territory to make their own decision concerning slavery was stated by; (Skill 1.7) (Rigorous)**

A. Henry Clay

B. Daniel Webster

C. John C. Calhoun

D. Stephen A. Douglas

36. Of the following groups of states, which were slave states?
(Skill 1.7) (Average)

   A. Delaware, Maryland, Missouri

   B. California, Texas, Florida

   C. Kansas, Missouri, Kentucky

   D. Virginia, West Virginia, Indiana

37. The Reconstruction period lasted from:
(Skill 1.7) (Rigorous)

   A. 1921 to 1938

   B. 1865 to 1900

   C. 1865 to 1877

   D. 1865 to 1917

38. In the American Civil War, who was the first commander of the forces of the United States?
(Skill 1.7) (Average)

   A. Gen. Ulysses S. Grant

   B. Gen. Robert E. Lee

   C. Gen. Irwin McDowell

   D. Gen. George Meade

39. How many states re-entered the Union before 1868?
(Skill 1.7) (Easy)

State	Date of Readmission
Alabama	1868
Arkansas	1868
Florida	1868
Georgia	1870
Louisiana	1868
Mississippi	1870
North Carolina	1868
South Carolina	1868
Tennessee	1866
Texas	1870
Virginia	1870

   A. 0 states

   B. 1 state

   C. 2 states

   D. 3 states

40. The post-Reconstruction was Not characterized by:
(Skill 1.7) (Average)

   A. Industrialization

   B. Growth of cities

   C. War

   D. Business boom

41. **What was not true of the pre-World War I United States?**
(Skill 1.7) (Rigorous)

   A. Isolationist

   B. Little influence on foreign Affairs

   C. Strong military force

   D. Weak military force

42. **The first explorer to arrive in Florida was:**
(Skill 1.8) (Rigorous)

   A. Christopher Columbus

   B. Panfilo de Narvaez

   C. Juan Ponce de Leon

   D. Hernando de Soto

43. **Which was not one of the five major Indian tribes in Florida?**
(Skill 1.8) (Easy)

   A. Calusa

   B. Hopi

   C. Ais

   D. Timucans

44. **The reason for the early exploration of Florida by Spain?**
(Skill 1.8) (Average)

   A. Establishment of missions

   B. Imperialism

   C. Establishment of settlements

   D. To find the fabled wealth of the Indians

45. **The French established a Settlement at:**
(Skill 1.8) (Rigorous)

   A. Ft. Caroline near Jacksonville

   B. Miami

   C. Pensacola

   D. There was no French Settlement

46. **Which country did not have a Presence in Florida?**
(Skill 1.8) (Easy)

   A. England

   B. France

   C. Spain

   D. Portugal

47. The first territorial governor of Florida after Florida's purchase by the United States was:
(Skill 1.8) (Rigorous)

   A. Napoleon B. Broward

   B. William P. Duval

   C. Andrew Jackson

   D. Davy Crockett

48. Which part of Florida were Plantations located in?
(Skill 1.8) (Rigorous)

   A. East Florida

   B. Middle Florida

   C. West Florida

   D. Southern Florida

49. What was the first governor of the State of Florida?
(Skill 1.8) (Average)

   A. Osceola

   B. Andrew Jackson

   C. David Levy Yulee

   D. William D. Mosley

50. Tourism to Florida began during the:
(Skill 1.9) (Rigorous)

   A. 1870s

   B 1860s

   C. 1890s

   D. 1900s

51. Economic development boomed in Southern Florida as early as:
(Skill 1.9) (Rigorous)

   A. 1850s

   B. 1860s

   C. 1900s

   D. 1950s

52. **Which of the following is most descriptive of the conflict between the U.S. government and the Seminoles between 1818 and 1858?**
(Skill 1.9) (Rigorous)

A. There was constant armed conflict between the Seminoles and the U.S. during these years

B. Historians discern three separate phases of hostilities (1818, 1835-42, 1855-58), known collectively as the Seminole Wars

C. On May 7, 1858, the Seminoles admitted defeat, signed a peace treaty with the U.S., and left for Oklahoma, except for fifty-one individuals

D. The former Seminole chief Osceola helped the U.S. defeat the Seminoles and effect their removal to Oklahoma

53. **Match the railroad entrepreneur with the correct area of development:**
(Skill 1.9) (Rigorous)

A. Henry Plant: Tampa and the West Coast

B. Cornelius Vanderbilt: Jacksonville and the Northeast

C. Henry Flagler: Orlando and the Central Highlands

D. J.P. Morgan: Pensacola and the Northwest

54. **Which industry is not a part of the Florida economy?**
(Skill 1.9) (Rigorous)

A. Paper

B. Electronics

C. Steel

D. Space and ocean exploration

55. **An area of lowlands formed by Soil and sediment at the Mouths of rivers is a (an):**
(Skill 2.1) (Rigorous)

A. Needle

B. Key

C. Delta

D. Mauna

56. Which is not on the North American continent:
(Skill 2.1) (Easy)

A. Mt. St. Helen's

B. The Himalayas

C. Mt. Everest

D. Pike's Peak

57. A physical geographer would be concerned with which of the following groups of terms?
(Skill 2.2) (Rigorous)

A. Low latitudes, precipitation, steppe

B. Scarcity, goods, services

C. Nation, state, administrative subdivision

D. Cause and effect, innovation, Exploration

58. What is a tundra?
(Skill 2.2) (Average)

A. A narrow ridge of sand, gravel, and boulders deposited by a stream flowing on, in, or under a nonmoving glacier

B. Accumulated earth, pebbles, and stones carried by and then deposited by a glacier

C. The active front face of a non-stagnant glacier

D. A marshy plain

59. Where are there only two Seasons?
(Skill 2.2) (Rigorous)

A. The Prairies

B. Savannas

C. The Middle latitudes

D. The Marine climate

60. Which of the following is NOT A type of climate:
(Skill 2.2) (Average)

A. Subtropical

B. Marine

C. Adiabatic

D. Vertical climate

61. The Mediterranean type climate is characterized by:
(Skill 2.2) (Average)

A. Hot, dry summers and mild, relatively wet winters

B. Cool, relatively wet summers and cold winters

C. Mild summers and winters, with moisture throughout the year

D. Hot, wet summers and cool, dry winters

62. The climate of Southern Florida is the

_____ type.
(Skill 2.2) (Easy)

A. Humid subtropical

B. Marine West Coast

C. Humid continental

D. Tropical wet-dry

63. Which is not a reason for different climate regions?
(Skill 2.2) (Easy)

A. Latitude

B. The amount of moisture

C. The time of day

D. Temperatures on land and water

64. We can credit modern geography with which of the following?
(Skill 2.3) (Average)

A. Building construction practices designed to withstand earthquakes

B. Advances in computer cartography

C. Better methods of linguistic analysis

D. Making it easier to memorize countries and their capitals

65. Which of the following is not A continent?
(Skill 2.3) (Easy)

A. Asia

B. Russia

C. Europe

D. North America

66. The continent of North America includes all but which of the following countries:
(Skill 2.3) (Easy)

A. Canada

B. Mexico

C. Cuba

D. Ecuador

67. **If geography is the study of how human beings live in relationship to the earth on which they live, why do geographers include physical geography within the discipline?**
    (Skill 2.4) (Average)

    A. The physical environment serves as the location for the activities of human beings

    B. No other branch of the natural or social sciences studies the same topics

    C. The physical environment is more important than the activities carried out by human beings

    D. It is important to be able to subdue natural processes for the advancement of humankind

68. **A cultural geographer is investigating the implications of The Return of the Native by Thomas Hardy. He or she is most likely concentrating on:**
    (Skill 2.4) (Rigorous)

    A. The reactions of British city-dwellers to the in-migration of French professionals

    B. The activities of persons in relation to poorly drained, coarse-soiled land with low-lying vegetation

    C. The capacity of riverine lands to sustain a population of edible amphibians

    D. The propagation of new crops introduced by settlers from North America

69. **Which of the following is not a concurrent power?**
    (Skill 3.2) (Average)

    A. Power to tax

    B. Power to declare war

    C. Power to borrow money

    D. Power to establish courts

70. Which of the following is not a branch of the federal government?
(Skill 3.2) (Easy)

   A. Executive

   B. Legislative

   C. Judicial

   D. Vehicle Registration

71. Which is not a power reserved to the states?
(Skill 3.2) (Average)

   A. To coin money

   B. To regulate intrastate trade

   C. Enacting state and local laws

   D. Establish local governments

72. Which of the following is (are) powers delegated to the federal government?
(Skill 3.2) (Average)

   A. To borrow and coin money

   B. To raise and support armed forces

   C. To fix standards of weights and standards

   D. All of these are powers delegated to the federal government

73. Which branch is responsible for carrying out the laws of the country?
(Skill 3.2) (Average)

   A. Judicial

   B. Executive

   C. Legislative

   D. Supreme Court

74. Which branch established the power of the Supreme Court?
(Skill 3.2) (Easy)

   A. Judicial

   B. Executive

   C. Legislative

   D. House of Representatives

75. The _____ branch of government is made up of House of Representatives and the Senate.
(Skill 3.2) (Easy)

   A. Judicial

   B. Executive

   C. Legislative

   D. Supreme Court

76. The nation's first political parties formed behind:
(Skill 3.2) (Rigorous)

   A. Washington and Hamilton

   B. Jefferson and Hamilton

   C. Madison and Hamilton

   D. Jefferson and Hamilton

77. Which one of the following is not a function or responsibility of the US political parties?
(Skill 3.2) (Average)

   A. Conducting elections or the voting process

   B. Obtaining funds needed for election campaigns

   C. Choosing candidates to run for public office

   D. Making voters aware of issues and other public affairs information

78. The U.S. Constitution, adopted in 1789, provided for:
(Skill 3.2) (Rigorous)

   A. Direct election of the President by all citizens

   B. Direct election of the President by citizens meeting a standard of wealth

   C. Indirect election of the President by electors

   D. Indirect election of the President by the U.S. Senate

79. In the Constitutional system of checks and balances, a primary "check" which accrues to the President is the power of:
(Skill 3.2) (Rigorous)

   A. Executive privilege

   B. Approval of judges nominated by the Senate

   C. Veto of Congressional legislation

   D. Approval of judged nominated by the House of Representatives

80. The Bill of Rights was mostly written by:
(Skill 3.4) (Rigorous)

   A. Thomas Jefferson

   B. James Madison

   C. George Washington

   D. Alexander Hamilton

81. Gerrymandering applies to:
(Skill 3.4) (Rigorous)

   A. All elections

   B. National elections

   C. Local elections

   D. Adjusting electoral districts to achieve a goal

82. In the Presidential Election of 1888, Grover Cleveland lost to Benjamin Harrison, although Cleveland received more popular votes. How is this possible?
(Skill 3.4) (Rigorous)

A. The votes of certain states (New York, Indiana) were thrown out because of voting irregularities

B. Harrison received more electoral votes than Cleveland

C. None of the party candidates received a majority of votes, and the House of Representatives elected Harrison according to Constitutional procedures

D. Because of accusations of election law violations, Cleveland withdrew his name and Harrison became President

83. What was not one of the factors leading to the American Revolution?
(Skill 3.6) (Average)

A. The desire to be an imperial Force

B. Belief in equality

C. Belief in no taxation without Representation

D. The desire for freedom

84. The term that best describes how the Supreme Court can block laws that may be unconstitutional from being enacted is:
(Skill 3.7) (Rigorous)

A. Jurisprudence

B. Judicial Review

C. Exclusionary Rule

D. Right of Petition

85. Which legislation promoted settlement in the West?
(Skill 3.7) (Average)

A. Quartering Act

B. Missouri Compromise

C. 1862 Homestead Act

D. Compromise of 1850

86. What Supreme Court ruling dealt with the issue of civil rights?
(Skill 3.8) (Average)

A. Jefferson vs Madison

B. Lincoln vs Douglas

C. Dred Scott v. Sanford

D. Marbury vs Madison

87. **Which concept is not embodied as a right in the First Amendment to the U.S. Constitution?**
(Skill 3.11) (Rigorous)

   A. Peaceable assembly

   B. Protection again unreasonable search and seizure

   C. Freedom of speech

   D. Petition for redress of Grievances

88. **According to the Constitution, any amendment must be ratified by _____ of the states to become a part of the Constitution:**
(Skill 3.11) (Average)

   A. Three-fourths

   B. Two-thirds

   C. Three-fifths

   D. Five-sixths

89. **Collectively, the first ten Amendments to the Constitution are known as the:**
(Skill 3.11) (Easy)

   A. Articles of Confederation

   B. Mayflower Compact

   C. Bill of Rights

   D. Declaration of the Rights of Man

90. **In the United States, if a person is accused of a crime and cannot afford a lawyer:**
(Skill 3.11) (Average)

   A. The person cannot be tried

   B. A court will appoint a lawyer, but the person must pay the lawyer back when able to do so

   C. The person must be tried without legal representation

   D. A court will appoint a lawyer for the person free of charge

91. **An amendment is:**
(Skill 3.11) (Easy)

   A. A change or addition to the United States Constitution

   B. The right of a state to secede from the Union

   C. To add a state to the Union

   D. The right of the Supreme Court to check actions of Congress and the President

92. **Which of the following is NOT considered to be a part of consumer economics:**
(Skill 4.1) (Average)

   A. Consumers

   B. Economic systems

   C. Consumer behavior

   D. Price

93. **Which best describes the economic system of the United States?**
(Skill 4.1) (Average)

A. Most decisions are the result of open markets, with little or no government modification or regulation

B. Most decisions are made by the government, but there is some input by open market forces

C. Most decisions are made by open market factors, with important regulatory functions and other market modifications the result of government activity

D. There is joint decision making by government and private forces, with final decisions resting with the government

94. **Capitalism and communism are alike in that they are both:**
(Skill 4.1 & 4.2) (Easy)

A. Organic systems

B. Political systems

C. Centrally planned systems

D. Economic systems

95. **In a Socialist or Communist economy:**
(Skill 4.2) (Average)

A. The open market determines how much of a good is produced and distributed

B. The government owns the means of production

C. Individuals produce and consume a specified good in whatever quantities they want

D. The open market determines the demand for a good, and then the government produces and distributes the good

96. **In a barter economy, which of the following would not be an economic factor?**
(Skill 4.2) (Easy)

A. Time

B. Goods

C. Money

D. Services

97. _____ is the effort to create, by dictatorial means, a viable national society in which competing interests were to be adjusted to each other by being entirely subordinated to the service of the state although it will tolerate some private ownership of the means of production.
(Skill 4.2) (Rigorous)

A. Dictatorship

B. Parliamentary System

C. Anarchism

D. Fascism

98. Which term does not apply to the stock market?
(Skill 4.3) (Average)

A. Bull market

B. Bear market

C. Investors

D. Black market

99. In a market economy, the price Of a good is affected by:
(Skill 4.3) (Easy)

A. Increase in demand and supply

B. Decrease in demand and Supply

C. Degree of competition

D. Prices are administered

100. Globalism refers to:
(Skill 4.4) (Easy)

A. Interdependence of all nations

B. Independence of all nations

C. Membership in the United Nations

D. Autarky

101. Which organization is concerned specifically with International trade?
(Skill 4.4) (Average)

A. NATO

B. United Nations

C. SEATO

D. WTO

102. Civics does not encompass:
(Skill 5.1) (Easy)

A. Rights and responsibilities of Citizens

B. Democracy

C. Interrelationships between people

D. Individual rights

103. Psychology is a social science because:
(Skill 5.1) (Easy)

A. It focuses on the biological development of individuals

B. It focuses on the behavior of individual persons and small groups of persons

C. It bridges the gap between the natural and the social sciences

D. It studies the behavioral habits of lower animals

104. A historian would be interested in:
(Skill 5.1) (Average)

A. The manner in which scientific knowledge is advanced

B. The effects of the French Revolution on world colonial policy

C. The viewpoint of persons who have written previous "history"

D. All of the above

105. The sub-discipline of linguistics is usually studied under:
(Skill 5.1) (Rigorous)

A. Geography

B. History

C. Anthropology

D. Economics

106. Which of the following is not generally considered to be a discipline within the social sciences?
(Skill 5.1) (Easy)

A. Geometry

B. Anthropology

C. Geography

D. Sociology

107. **Economics is best described as:**
(Skill 5.1) (Average)

A. The study of how money is used in different societies

B. The study of how different political systems produce goods and services

C. The study of how human beings use limited resources to supply their necessities and wants

D. The study of how human beings have developed trading practices through the years

108. **Which of the following is most reasonably studied under the social sciences?**
(Skill 5.1) (Easy)

A. Political science

B. Geometry

C. Physics

D. Grammar

109. **Which is not a main division of history?**
(Skill 5.1) (Rigorous)

A. Time periods

B. Nations

C. Specialized topics

D. Relationship to culture

110. **A political scientist might use all of the following except:**
(Skill 5.1)(Rigorous)

A. An investigation of government documents

B. A geological timeline

C. Voting patterns

D. Polling data

111. **A geographer wishes to study the effects of a flood on subsequent settlement patterns. Which might he or she find most useful?**
(Skill 5.1)(Rigorous)

A. A film clip of the floodwaters

B. An aerial photograph of the river's source

C. Census data taken after the flood

D. A soil map of the A and B horizons beneath the flood area

112. **A social scientist observes how individual persons react to the presence or absence of noise. This scientist is most likely a:**
(Skill 5.1) (Average)

A. Geographer

B. Political Scientist

C. Economist

D. Psychologist

113. **As a sociologist, you would be most likely to observe: (Skill 5.1) (Easy)**

    A. The effects of an earthquake on farmland

    B. The behavior of rats in sensory-deprivation experiments

    C. The change over time in Babylonian obelisk styles

    D. The behavior of human beings in television focus groups

114. **Which name is not associated with economics? (Skill 5.1) (Average)**

    A. Adam Smith

    B. John Stuart Mill

    C. John Maynard Keynes

    D. Edward Gibbon

115. **Cognitive, developmental, and behavioral are three types of: (Skill 5.1) (Average)**

    A. Economists

    B. Political Scientists

    C. Psychologists

    D. Historians

116. **An economist might engage in which of the following activities? (Skill 5.1) (Rigorous)**

    A. An observation of the historical effects of a nation's banking practices

    B. The application of a statistical test to a series of data

    C. Introduction of an experimental factor into a specified population to measure the effect of the factor

    D. An economist might engage in all of these

117. **Political science is primarily concerned with _____. (Skill 5.1) (Easy)**

    A. Elections

    B. Economic Systems

    C. Boundaries

    D. Public Policy

118. A social scientist studies the behavior of four persons in a carpool. This is an example of: (Skill 5.1) (Average)

    A. Developmental psychology

    B. Experimental psychology

    C. Social psychology

    D. Macroeconomics

119. A teacher and a group of students take a field trip to an Indian mound to examine artifacts. This activity most closely fits under which branch of the social sciences?
    (Skill 5.1) (Average)

    A. Anthropology

    B. Sociology

    C. Psychology

    D. Political Science

120. Which of the following is most closely identified as a sociologist?
    (Skill 5.1) (Rigorous)

    A. Herodotus

    B. John Maynard Keynes

    C. Emile Durkheim

    D. Arnold Toynbee

121. Adam Smith is most closely identified with which of the following?
    (Skill 5.1) (Average)

    A. The law of diminishing returns

    B. The law of supply and demand

    C. The principle of motor primacy

    D. The territorial imperative

122. Margaret Mead may be credited with major advances in the study of:
    (Skill 5.1) (Average)

    A. The marginal propensity to consume

    B. The thinking of the Anti-Federalists

    C. The anxiety levels of non-human primates

    D. Interpersonal relationships in non-technical societies

123. Of the following lists, which includes persons who have made major advances in the understanding of psychology?
(Skill 5.1) (Rigorous)

   A. Herodotus, Thucydides, Ptolemy

   B. Adam Smith, Milton Friedman, John Kenneth Galbraith

   C. Edward Hall, E.L. Thorndike, B.F. Skinner

   D. Thomas Jefferson, Karl Marx, Henry Kissinger

124. The advancement of understanding in dealing with human beings has led to a number of interdisciplinary areas. Which of the following interdisciplinary studies would NOT be considered under the social sciences?
(Skill 5.1) (Average)

   A. Molecular biophysics

   B. Peace studies

   C. African-American studies

   D. Cartographic information systems

125. An anthropologist is studying a society's sororate and avunculate. In general, this scientist is studying the society's:
(Skill 5.1) (Rigorous)

   A. Level of technology

   B. Economy

   C. Kinship practices

   D. Methods of farming

Answer Key

1.	C	34.	D	67.	A	100.	A
2.	A	35.	D	68.	B	101.	D
3	C	36.	A	69.	B	102.	C
4.	C	37.	C	70.	D	103.	B
5.	A	38.	C	71.	A	104.	D
6.	D	39.	B	72.	D	105.	C
7.	B	40.	C	73.	B	106.	A
8.	D	41.	C	74.	A	107.	C
9.	B	42.	C	75.	C	108.	A
10.	C	43.	B	76.	B	109.	D
11.	B	44.	D	77.	A	110.	B
12.	B	45.	A	78.	C	111.	C
13.	C	46.	D	79.	C	112.	D
14.	C	47.	C	80.	B	113.	D
15.	C	48.	B	81.	D	114.	D
16.	D	49.	D	82.	B	115.	C
17.	B	50.	A	83.	A	116.	D
18.	A	51.	C	84.	B	117.	D
19.	A	52.	B	85.	C	118.	C
20.	B	53.	A	86.	C	119.	A
21.	D	54.	C	87.	B	120.	C
22.	A	55.	C	88.	A	121.	B
23.	C	56.	B	89.	C	122.	D
24.	C	57.	A	90.	D	123.	C
25.	A	58.	D	91.	A	124.	A
26.	B	59.	B	92.	B	125.	C
27.	B	60.	C	93.	C		
28.	B	61.	A	94.	D		
29.	D	62.	A	95.	B		
30.	A	63.	C	96.	C		
31.	B	64.	B	97.	D		
32.	D	65.	B	98.	D		
33.	D	66.	D	99.	D		

Rigor Table

Easy (20%)	Average Rigor (40%)	Rigorous (40%)
1, 17, 39, 41, 43, 46, 56, 62, 63, 65, 66, 70, 74, 75, 89, 91, 94, 96, 99, 100, 102, 103, 106, 108, 113, 117	2, 6, 7, 10, 11, 13, 14, 19, 20, 23, 24, 27, 28, 30, 31, 36, 38, 40, 44, 49, 58, 60, 61, 64, 67, 69, 71, 72, 73, 77, 83, 85, 86, 88, 90, 92, 93, 95, 98, 101, 104, 107, 112, 114, 115, 118, 119, 121, 122, 124	3, 4, 5, 8, 9, 12, 15, 16, 18, 21, 22, 25, 26, 29, 32, 33, 34, 35, 37, 41, 42, 45, 47, 48, 50, 51, 52, 53, 54, 57, 59, 68, 76, 78, 79, 80, 81, 82, 84, 87, 97, 105, 109, 110, 111, 116, 120, 121, 123, 125

Rationales with Sample Questions

1. **The important issues in the 20th century were:**
   (Skill 1.1) (Easy)

   A. Political

   B. Economic

   C. Historical

   D. Social

Answer: C. Historical

The major issues of the 20th century were political, economic and social. Historical issues don't really enter into it.

2. **The Age of Exploration begun in the 1400s was led by:**
   (Skill 1.1) (Average)

   A. The Portuguese

   B. The Spanish

   C. The English

   D. The Dutch

Answer: A. The Portuguese

Although the Age of Exploration had many important players among them, the Dutch, Spanish and English, it was the Portuguese who sent the first explorers to the New World.

3. **Bartholomeu Dias, in seeking a route around the tip of Africa, was forced to turn back. Nevertheless, the cape he discovered near the southern tip of Africa became known as:**
    (Skill 1.1) (Rigorous)

    A. Cape Horn

    B. Cabo Bojador

    C. Cape of Good Hope

    D. Cape Hatteras

Answer: C. Cape of Good Hope

(A) Cape Horn is located at the southern tip of Chile, and therefore South America. It was discovered by Sir Francis Drake as he sailed around the globe in 1578. (B) Cajo Bojador, on the Western coast of northern Africa, was first successfully navigated by a European, Portuguese Gil Eanes, in 1434. (D) Cape Hatteras is located on the U.S. Atlantic coast, at North Carolina.

4. **Which of the following developments is most closely associated with the Neolithic Age?**
    (Skill 1.1) (Rigorous)

    A. Human use of fire

    B. First use of stone chipping instruments

    C. Domestication of animals

    D. Development of metallurgical alloys

Answer: C. Domestication of animals

The Neolithic or "New Stone" Age, as its name implies, is characterized by the use of stone implements, but the first use of stone chipping instruments appears in the Paleolithic period. Human use of fire may go back still farther and certainly predates the Neolithic era. The Neolithic period is distinguished by the domestication of plants and animals. The development of metallurgical alloys marks the conclusion of the Neolithic Age.

5. **Which does not apply to the ancient Assyrians?**
   (Skill 1.1) (Rigorous)

   A. Developed maps

   B. Warlike

   C. Organized military

   D. Horse Drawn Chariots

Answer: A. Developed maps

The ancient Assyrians were (B) warlike, (C) had an organized military and (D) used horse drawn chariots. They did not (A) develop maps.

6. **Which of the following is not a religion of China:**
   (Skill 1.3) (Average)

   A. Confucianism

   B. Taoism

   C. Buddhism

   D. Shintoism

Answer: D. Shintoism

(A) Confucianism, (B) Taoism and (C) Buddhism are all religions of China. (D) Shintoism is a religion of Japan.

7.   **The first ancient civilization to introduce and practice monotheism was the:**
     (Skill 1.3) (Average)

     A. Sumerians

     B. Hebrews

     C. Phoenicians

     D. Minoans

Answer: B. Hebrews

The (A) Sumerians and (C) Phoenicians both practiced religions in which many gods and goddesses were worshipped. Often these Gods/Goddesses were based on a feature of nature such as a sun, moon, weather, rocks, water, etc. The (D) Minoan culture shared many religious practices with the Ancient Egyptians. It seems that the king was somewhat of a god figure and the queen, a goddess. Much of the Minoan art points to the worship of multiple gods. Therefore, only the (B) Hebrews introduced and fully practiced monotheism, or the belief in one god.

8.   **Which of the following is not a result of the Industrial Revolution?**
     (Skill 1.4) (Rigorous)

     A. Growth of cities

     B. Increased productivity

     C. Specialization and division of labor

     D. Rise in religious tolerance

Answer: D. Rise in religious tolerance

The Industrial Revolution resulted in machinery and better production techniques which resulted in increased jobs and output. The increased output was due to (B) increased productivity and (C) the specialization and division of labor. This led to (A) the growth of cities and people migrated for better jobs. The Industrial Revolution had nothing to do with (D) a rise in religious tolerance.

9. **The area of the United States was effectively doubled through purchase of the Louisiana Territory under which President? (Skill 1.4) (Rigorous)**

    A. John Adams

    B. Thomas Jefferson

    C. James Madison

    D. James Monroe

Answer: B. Thomas Jefferson

(B) The Louisiana Purchase, an acquisition of territory from France, in 1803 occurred under Thomas Jefferson. (A) John Adams (1735-1826) was president from 1797-1801, before the purchase, and (C) James Madison, (1751-1836) after the Purchase (1809-1817). (D) James Monroe (1758-1831) was actually a signatory on the Purchase but also did not become President until 1817.

10. **The politics of classical Athens is best described by which of the following? (Skill 1.5) (Average)**

    A. Limited democracy, including both slaves and free men

    B. One man dictatorial rule

    C. Universal democracy among free owners of property

    D. Oligarchy with a few families controlling all decisions

Answer: C. Universal democracy among free owners of property.

A citizen of Athens was a free man who owned property. Each had an equal vote in the governance of the city. All the other answers are thereby excluded by definition.

11. **The Pax Romana resulted in all but the following:**
    (Skill 1.5) (Average)

    A. Free travel and trade

    B. The Punic Wars

    C. Expansion of Culture

    D. A long period of peace

Answer: B. The Punic Wars

The Pax Romana was a long period of peace. Therefore, the Punic Wars were not during that period.

12. **Secularism was the most significant aspect of all but the following civilizations:**
    (Skill 1.5) (Rigorous)

    A. Greek

    B. Sumerian

    C. Hellenic

    D. Roman

Answer: B. Sumerian

The (B) Sumerian civilization preceded the civilizations of Greek, Hellenic and Roman. Secularism was important to all but the Sumerians.

13. **The Compromise of 1850 came about as a result of which state's entry into the Union?**
(Skill 1.5) (Average)

A. Texas

B. Missouri

C. California

D. Kansas

Answer: C. California

Texas (A) entered the Union in 1845. Missouri (B) was the subject of the Missouri Compromise of 1824, which would be the first such compromise between slave and free states. California (C) entered the union after the Compromise of 1850 was drafted to avoid the issue of secession by the slave states. Kansas (D) became a violent battleground between pro-slavery and anti-slavery forces when it was organized as a territory in 1854, before achieving statehood in 1861 as a free state.

14. **The last Czar of Russia was:**
(Skill 1.6) (Average)

A. Peter the Great

B. Ivan the Terrible

C. Nicholas II

D. Catherine the Great

Answer: C. Nicholas II

Nicholas II was the last in the line of Russian Czars and was assassinated after the Revolution took place.

15. **Chinese civilization is generally credited with the original development of which of the following sets of technologies: (Skill 1.6) (Rigorous)**

A. Movable type and mass production of goods

B. Wool processing and domestication of the horse

C. Paper and gunpowder manufacture

D. Leather processing and modern timekeeping

Answer: C. Paper and gunpowder manufacture

(A) While China's Bi Sheng (d. 1052) is credited with the earliest forms of movable type (1041-48), mass production was spearheaded by America's Henry Ford (1863-1947) in his campaign to create the first truly affordable automobile, the Model T Ford. (B) While wool has been processed in many ways in many cultures, production on a scale beyond cottage industries was not possible without the many advances made in England during the Industrial Revolution (18th century). Various theories exist about the domestication of the horse, with estimates ranging from 4600 BC to 2000 BC in Eurasia. Recent DNA evidence suggests that the horse may actually have been domesticated in different cultures at independent points. (C) The earliest mention of gunpowder appears in ninth century Chinese documents. The earliest examples of paper made of wood pulp come from China and have been dated as early as the second century BC. (D) Leather processing and timekeeping have likewise seen different developments in different places at different times.

16.   **Which was not one of the five major tribes of the Middle Ages? (Skill 1.6) (Rigorous)**

  A. Visigoths

  B. Saxons

  C. Vandals

  D. Phoenicians

Answer: D. Phoenicians

The (A) Visigoths, (B) Saxons and (C) Vandals were part of the five major tribes of the Middle Ages. The Phoenicians existed in a much earlier age.

17.   **The painter of the Sistine Ceiling was: (Skill 1.6) (Easy)**

  A. Raphael

  B. Michelangelo

  C. Leonardo da Vinci

  D. Titian

Answer: B. Michelangelo

(A) Raphael (1483-1520 AD), (B) Michelangelo (1475-1564 AD), (C) Leonardo da Vinci (1452-1519 AD) and (D) Titian (1488-1576 AD) were all contemporary Italian Renaissance masters, but only Michelangelo painted the Sistine Chapel ceiling (1508-1512 AD).

18.   **Church abuses leading to the Protestant Revolution included all but:**
      (Skill 1.6) (Rigorous)

      A. Disagreement over the role of Jesus Christ

      B. Sale of dispensations

      C. The sale of indulgences, whereby the buyer may purchase purgation of Sins

      D. Fraudulent clergy

Answer: A. Disagreement over the role of Jesus Christ

Absolution of sins by priests, the sale of indulgences and imposed church control over individual consciences were all practices which Martin Luther (1483-1546) and subsequent Protestants objected to on the basis that they required the Church to act as an intermediary between God and the individual believer. The role of Jesus Christ was not disputed.

19.   **The Renaissance began in:**
      (Skill 1.6) (Average)

      A. Florence

      B. Greece

      C. England

      D. France

Answer: A. Florence

Florence was the birthplace of the Renaissance.

20. **The first explorer to reach India by sailing around the southern tip of Africa was:**
(Skill 1.6) (Average)

   A. Amerigo Vespucci

   B. Vasco da Gama

   C. Ferdinand Magellan

   D. John Cabot

Answer: B. Vasco da Gama

(A) Amerigo Vespucci (1454-1512) was the Italian explorer to first assert that the lands to the west of Africa and Europe were actually part of a new continent and thus the name "America" was derived from his own "Amerigo." (B) Portuguese Vasco da Gama (1469-1524) built on the discoveries of previous explorers to finally round Africa's Cape of Good Hope and open a sea route for European trade with the east and the eventual Portuguese colonization of India. (C) Portuguese explorer Ferdinand Magellan (1480-1521), working for the Spanish crown, led the first successful expedition to circumnavigate the globe (1519-1522). Magellan himself actually died before the voyage was over, but his ship and 18 crewmembers did return safely to Spain. (D) John Cabot (1450-1499) was an Italian explorer working for the English crown and is thought to have been the first European to discover North America (1497) since the Vikings.

21. **Great Britain became the center of technological and industrial development during the nineteenth century chiefly on the basis of: (Skill 1.6) (Rigorous)**

    A. Central location relative to the population centers of Europe

    B. Colonial conquests and military victories over European powers

    C. Reliance on exterior sources of financing

    D. Resources of coal and production of steel

Answer: D. Resources of coal and production of steel

Great Britain possessed a unique set of advantages in the 18th and 19th century, making it the perfect candidate for the technological advances of the Industrial Revolution. (A) Relative isolation from the population centers in Europe meant little to Great Britain, which benefited from its own relatively unified and large domestic market, enabling it to avoid the tariffs and inefficiencies of trading on the diverse (and complicated) continent. (B) Colonial conquests and military victories over European powers were fueled by Great Britain's industrial advances in transportation and weaponry, rather than being causes of them. (C) Reliance on exterior sources of funding – while Great Britain would enjoy an increasing influx of goods and capital from its colonies, the efficiency of its own domestic market consistently generated an impressive amount of capital for investment in the new technologies and industries of the age. (D) Great Britain's rich natural resources of coal and ore enabled steel production and, set alongside new factories in a Britain's landscape, allowed the production of goods quickly and efficiently.

22. **Which of the following is not associated with the Age of Exploration? (Skill 1.6) (Rigorous)**

    A. The need for food

    B. The Vivaldo Brothers

    C. Marco Polo

    D. The quest for trade routes

Answer: A. The need for food

The need for food was not a reason or a name associated with the Age of Exploration.

23. **Which revolution occurred the latest: (Skill 1.6) (Average)**

    A. American Revolution

    B. French Revolution

    C. Chinese Revolution

    D. Russian Revolution

Answer: C. Chinese Revolution

Chronically, the Chinese Revolution occurred the latest.

24. **The belief that the United States should control all of North America was called:**
(Skill 1.7) (Average)

A. Westward Expansion

B. Pan Americanism

C. Manifest Destiny

D. Nationalism

Answer: C. Manifest Destiny

The belief that the United States should control all of North America was called (B) Manifest Destiny. This idea fueled much of the violence and aggression towards those already occupying the lands such as the Native Americans. Manifest Destiny was certainly driven by sentiments of (D) nationalism and gave rise to (A) westward expansion.

25. **Of all the major causes of both World Wars I and II, the most significant one is considered to be:**
   (Skill 1.7) (Rigorous)

   A. Extreme nationalism

   B. Military buildup and aggression

   C. Political unrest

   D. Agreements and alliances

Answer: A. Extreme nationalism

Although military buildup and aggression, political unrest, and agreements and alliances were all characteristic of the world climate before and during World War I and World War II, the most significant cause of both wars was extreme nationalism. Nationalism is the idea that the interests and needs of a particular nation are of the utmost and primary importance above all else. Some nationalist movements could be liberation movements while others were oppressive regimes, much depends on their degree of nationalism. The nationalism that sparked WWI included a rejection of German, Austro-Hungarian, and Ottoman imperialism by Serbs, Slavs and others culminating in the assassination of Archduke Ferdinand by a Serb nationalist in 1914. Following WWI and the Treaty of Versailles, many Germans and others in the Central Alliance Nations, malcontent at the concessions and reparations of the treaty started a new form of nationalism. Adolf Hitler and the Nazi regime led this extreme nationalism. Hitler's ideas were an example of extreme, oppressive nationalism combined with political, social and economic scapegoating and were the primary cause of WWII.

26. **Leaders in the movement for woman's rights have included all but:**
(Skill 1.7) (Rigorous)

A. Elizabeth Cady Stanton

B. Lucretia Borgia

C. Susan B. Anthony

D. Lucretia Mott

Answer: B. Lucretia Borgia

The only name not associated with the woman's rights movement is Lucretia Borgia. The others were all pioneers in the movement with Susan B. Anthony and Elizabeth Cady Stanton being the founders of the National Woman Suffrage Association in 1869.

27. **The Middle Colonies of the Americas were:**
(Skill 1.7) (Average)

A. Maryland, Virginia, North Carolina

B. New York, New Jersey, Pennsylvania, Delaware

C. Rhode Island, Connecticut, New York, New Jersey

D. Vermont and New Hampshire

Answer: B. New York, New Jersey, Pennsylvania, Delaware

(A), (C) & (D). Maryland, Virginia, and North Carolina were Southern colonies, Rhode Island, Connecticut ,and New Hampshire were New England colonies and Vermont was not one of the 13 original colonies.

28. **Slavery arose in the Southern Colonies partly as a perceived economical way to:**
    (Skill 1.7) (Average)

    A. Increase the owner's wealth through human beings used as a source of exchange

    B. Cultivate large plantations of cotton, tobacco, rice, indigo, and other crops

    C. Provide Africans with humanitarian aid, such as health care, Christianity, and literacy

    D. Keep ships' holds full of cargo on two out of three legs of the "triangular trade" voyage

Answer: B. Cultivate large plantations of cotton, tobacco, rice, indigo, and other crops.

The Southern states, with their smaller populations, were heavily dependent on slave labor as a means of being able to fulfill their role and remain competitive in the greater U.S. economy. (A) When slaves arrived in the South, the vast majority would become permanent fixtures on plantations, intended for work, not as a source of exchange. (C) While some slave owners instructed their slaves in Christianity, provided health care or some level of education, such attention was not their primary reason for owning slaves – a cheap and ready labor force was. (D) Whether or not ships' holds were full on two or three legs of the triangular journey was not the concern of Southerners as the final purchasers of slaves. Such details would have concerned the slave traders.

29. **France decided in 1777 to help the American colonies in their war against Britain. This decision was based on:**
(Skill 1.7) (Rigorous)

   A. The naval victory of John Paul Jones over the British ship Serapis"

   B. The survival of the terrible winter at Valley Forge

   C. The success of colonial guerilla fighters in the South

   D. The defeat of the British at Saratoga

Answer: D. The defeat of the British at Saratoga

The turning point in the Americans' favor occurred in 1777 with the (D) American victory at Saratoga. This victory decided for the French to align themselves with the Americans against the British. With the aid of French warships blocking the entrance to Chesapeake Bay, British General Cornwallis trapped at Yorktown, Virginia, surrendered in 1781 and the war was over.

30. **A major quarrel between colonial Americans and the British concerned a series of British Acts of Parliament dealing with: (Skill 1.7) (Average)**

   A. Taxes

   B. Slavery

   C. Native Americans

   D. Shipbuilding

Answer: A. Taxes

Acts of Parliament imposing taxes on the colonists always provoked resentment. Because the colonies had no direct representation in Parliament, they felt it unjust that that body should impose taxes on them, with so little knowledge of their very different situation in America and no real concern for the consequences of such taxes. (B) While slavery continued to exist in the colonies long after it had been completely abolished in Britain, it never was a source of serious debate between Britain and the colonies. By the time Britain outlawed slavery in its colonies in 1833, the American Revolution had already taken place and the United States were free of British control. (C) There was no series of British Acts of Parliament passed concerning Native Americans. (D) Colonial shipbuilding was an industry that received little interference from the British.

31.   The first shots in what was to become the American Revolution were fired in:
(Skill 1.7) (Average)

   A. Florida

   B. Massachusetts

   D. New York

   D. Virginia

Answer: B. Massachusetts

(A) At the time of the American Revolution, Florida, while a British possession, was not directly involved in the Revolutionary War. (B) The American Revolution began with the battles of Lexington and Concord in 1775. (C) There would be no fighting in New York until 1776 and none in Virginia until 1781.

32.   Of the following, which contributed most to penetration of western areas by colonial Americans?
(Skill 1.7) (Rigorous)

   A. Development of large ships capable of sailing upstream in rivers such as the Hudson, Susquehanna, and Delaware

   B. The invention of the steamboat

   C. Improved relations with Native Americans, who invited colonial Americans to travel west to settle

   D. Improved roads, mail service, and communications

Answer: D. Improved roads, mail service and communications

(A) Because the Susquehanna, Delaware, and Hudson are limited to the northeast, they would not have helped the colonists penetrate any further West. (B) Since these were the waterways that they had immediate access to, the development of the steamboat was similarly unhelpful in this regard. (C) In general, colonist-Native American relations got worse, not better as colonists moved West, so colonists were unlikely to have been invited yet further west. (D) Improved roads, mail service, and communications made traveling west easier and more.

33. **What was a major source of contention between American settlers in Texas and the Mexican government in the 1830s and 1840s?**
(Skill 1.7) (Rigorous)

   A. The Americans wished to retain slavery, which had been outlawed in Mexico

   B. The Americans had agreed to learn Spanish and become Roman Catholic, but failed to do so

   C. The Americans retained ties to the United States, and Santa Anna feared the power of the U.S.

   D. All of the above were contentious issues between American settlers And the Mexican government

Answer: D. All of the above were contentious issues between American settlers and the Mexican government.

The American settlers simply were not willing to assimilate into Mexican society but maintained their prior commitments to slave holding, the English language, Protestantism, and the United States government.

34. **A consequence of the Gold Rush of Americans to California in 1848 and 1849 was that:**
(Skill 1.7) (Rigorous)

   A. California spent the minimum amount of time as a territory, and was admitted as a slave state

   B. California was denied admission on its first application, since most Americans felt that the settlers were too "uncivilized" to deserve statehood

   C. California was purchased from Mexico for the express purpose of gaining immediate statehood

   D. California did not go through the normal territorial stage but applied directly for statehood as a free state

Answer: D. California did not go through the normal territorial stage but applied directly for statehood as a free state.

California, suddenly undergoing a massive increase in population and wealth and desiring orderly government, found it had little recourse but to claim status as a free state and appeal directly for statehood. Congress had moved too slowly on the question of making California United States Territory. California was never a territory but only a military district. California was not denied admission to the Union but was an essential part of the Compromise of 1850. Immediate statehood was definitely not an express policy of the U.S. in acquiring California, but the Gold Rush changed attitudes quickly.

35. The principle of "popular sovereignty" allowing people in any territory to make their own decision concerning slavery was stated by;
(Skill 1.7) (Rigorous)

A. Henry Clay

B. Daniel Webster

C. John C. Calhoun

D. Stephen A. Douglas

Answer: D. Stephen A. Douglas

(A) Henry Clay (1777-1852) and (B) Daniel Webster (1782-1852) were prominent Whigs whose main concern was keeping the United States one nation. They opposed Andrew Jackson and his Democratic party around the 1830s in favor of promoting what Clay called "the American System". (C) John C. Calhoun (1782-1850) served as Vice-President under John Quincy Adams and Andrew Jackson, and then as a state senator from South Carolina. He was very pro-slavery and a champion of states' rights. The principle of "popular sovereignty", in which people in each territory could make their own decisions concerning slavery, was the doctrine of (D) Stephen A. Douglas (1813-1861). Douglas was looking for a middle ground between the abolitionists of the North and the pro-slavery Democrats of the South. However, as the polarization of pro- and anti-slavery sentiments grew, he lost the presidential election to Republican Abraham Lincoln, who later abolished slavery.

36.   **Of the following groups of states, which were slave states? (Skill 1.7) (Average)**

A. Delaware, Maryland, Missouri

B. California, Texas, Florida

C. Kansas, Missouri, Kentucky

D. Virginia, West Virginia, Indiana

Answer: A. Delaware, Maryland, Missouri.

(A) Delaware, Maryland and Missouri were all slave states at the time of the Civil War. (B) Florida and Texas were slave states, while California was a free state. (C) Kansas, Missouri, and Kentucky were all originally slave territories, and Missouri and Kentucky were admitted to the Union as such. However, Kansas' petition to join the union in 1858 was blocked in order to preserve the balance between slave and free states. Kansas was admitted as a free state in 1861. (D) Indiana was a free state.

37.   The Reconstruction period lasted from:
       (Skill 1.7) (Rigorous)

       A. 1921 to 1938

       B. 1865 to 1900

       C. 1865 to 1877

       D. 1865 to 1917

Answer: C. 1865 to 1877

The Reconstruction period concerned the rebuilding of the South in the years following the Civil War and lasted from 1865 until 1877.

38.   In the American Civil War, who was the first commander of the forces of the United States?
       (Skill 1.7) (Average)

       A. Gen. Ulysses S. Grant

       B. Gen. Robert E. Lee

       C. Gen. Irwin McDowell

       D. Gen. George Meade

Answer: C. General Irwin McDowell

(A) Gen. Ulysses S. Grant was the final commander of the Union army during the Civil War. (B) Gen. Robert E. Lee was the commander of the Confederate army. (D) Gen. George Meade was the Union commander at the Battle of Gettysburg in 1863.

39. **How many states re-entered the Union before 1868?**
    (Skill 1.7) (Easy)

State	Date of Readmission
Alabama	1868
Arkansas	1868
Florida	1868
Georgia	1870
Louisiana	1868
Mississippi	1870
North Carolina	1868
South Carolina	1868
Tennessee	1866
Texas	1870
Virginia	1870

    A. 0 states

    B. 1 state

    C. 2 states

    D. 3 states

Answer: B. 1 state

Only Tennessee was readmitted before 1868, as the above table indicates.

40. **The post-Reconstruction was characterized by:**
(Skill 1.7) (Average)

   A. Industrialization

   B. Growth of cities

   C. War

   D. Bussiness boom

Answer: C. War

The post-Reconsruction years were periods of prosperity. It was the time of industrialization, the growth of cities and a tremendous business boom. War wa not a part of this period.

41. **What was not true of the pre- World War I United States?**
(Skill 1.7) (Rigorous)

   A. Isolationist

   B. Little influence on foreign
   Affairs

   C. Strong military force

   D. Weak military force

Answer: C. Strong military force

The United States did not have a (C) strong military force. They were rather weak militarily but mobilized for the war effort.

42. **The first explorer to arrive in Florida was:**
(Skill 1.8) (Rigorous)

A. Christopher Columbus

B. Panfilo de Narvaez

C. Juan Ponce de Leon

D. Hernando de Soto

Answer: C. Juan Ponce de Leon

Juan Ponce de Leon arrived in Florida in 1513 searching for the Fountain of Youth. He was the first of the Spanish explorers.

43. **Which was not one of the five major Indian tribes in Florida?**
(Skill 1.8) (Easy)

A. Calusa

B. Hopi

C. Ais

D. Timucans

Answer: B. Hopi

When Europeans eventually arrived, there were about 10,000 Indians belonging to as many as five major tribes. In the south, were the Calusa and the Tequesta; the Ais were found on the Atlantic coast in the central part of the peninsula; the Timucans were in the central and northeast area of the state; and in the northwest part of Florida dwelled the Apalachee. (B) The Hopi are a tribe in the American Southwest.

44. **The reason for the early exploration of Florida by Spain?**
    (Skill 1.8) (Average)

    A. Establishment of missions

    B. Imperialism

    C. Establishment of settlements

    D. To find the fabled wealth of the Indians

Answer: D. To find the fabled wealth of the Indians

The Indians were thought to have a great deal of wealth and this is what attracted the early settlers.

45. **The French established a Settlement at:**
    (Skill 1.8) (Rigorous)

    A. Ft. Caroline near Jacksonville

    B. Miami

    C. Pensacola

    D. There was no French Settlement

Answer: A. Ft. Caroline near Jacksonville

The first French settlement was in 1564 at Fort Caroline.

46. **Which country did not have a presence in Florida?**
    (Skill 1.8) (Easy)

    A. England

    B. France

    C. Spain

    D. Portugal

Answer: D. Portugal

England, France and Spain were the early settlers of Florida. (D) Portugal was not.

47. **The first territorial governor of Florida after Florida's purchase by the United States was:**
    (Skill 1.8) (Rigorous)

    A. Napoleon B. Broward

    B. William P. Duval

    C. Andrew Jackson

    D. Davy Crockett

Answer: C. Andrew Jackson

Andrew Jackson became the territorial governor in 1821.

48. **Which part of Florida were Plantations located in?**
(Skill 1.8) (Rigorous)

    A. East Florida

    B. Middle Florida

    C. West Florida

    D. Southern Florida

Answer: B. Middle Florida

Florida now was divided informally into three areas: East Florida, from the Atlantic Ocean to the Suwannee River; Middle Florida, between the Suwannee and the Apalachicola Rivers; and West Florida, from the Apalachicola to the Perdido River. The southern area of the territory (south of present-day Gainesville) was sparsely settled by whites. The territory's economy was based on agriculture. Plantations were concentrated in Middle Florida, and their owners established the political tone for all of Florida until after the Civil War.

49. **What was the first governor of the State of Florida?**
(Skill 1.8) (Average)

    A. Osceola

    B. Andrew Jackson

    C. David Levy Yulee

    D. William D. Mosley

Answer: D. William D. Mosley

Florida became the twenty-seventh state in the United States on March 3, 1845. William D. Mosley was elected the new state's first governor.

50. **Tourism to Florida began during the:**
(Skill 1.9) (Rigorous)

    A. 1870s

    B 1860s

    C. 1890s

    D. 1900s

Answer: A. 1870s

Florida became a vacation haven after the Civil War, in the 1870s. People from other parts of the country were attracted by the climate.

51. **Economic development boomed in Southern Florida as early as:**
(Skill 1.9) (Rigorous)

    A. 1850s

    B. 1860s

    C. 1900s

    D. 1950s

Answer: C. 1900s

Economic development boomed around the turn of the century.

52. **Which of the following is most descriptive of the conflict between the U.S. government and the Seminoles between 1818 and 1858? (Skill 1.9) (Rigorous)**

   A. There was constant armed conflict between the Seminoles and the U.S. during these years

   B. Historians discern three separate phases of hostilities (1818, 1835-42, 1855-58), known collectively as the Seminole Wars

   C. On May 7, 1858, the Seminoles admitted defeat, signed a peace treaty with the U.S., and left for Oklahoma, except for fifty-one individuals

   D. The former Seminole chief Osceola helped the U.S. defeat the Seminoles and effect their removal to Oklahoma

Answer: B. Historians discern three separate phases of hostilities (1818, 1835-42, 1855-58), known collectively as the Seminole Wars.

(A) Intermittent conflicts between the U.S. government and the Seminole Native Americans can be classified into (B) three separate phases of hostilities. (C)

53. **Match the railroad entrepreneur with the correct area of development: (Skill 1.9) (Rigorous)**

   A. Henry Plant: Tampa and the West Coast

   B. Cornelius Vanderbilt: Jacksonville and the Northeast

   C. Henry Flagler: Orlando and the Central Highlands

   D. J.P. Morgan: Pensacola and the Northwest

Answer: A. Henry Plant: Tampa and the West Coast

(A) Henry Plant (1819-1899) was responsible for building railroad along the West Coast of Florida, making Tampa the end of the line. (B) Cornelius Vanderbilt (1794-1877), transportation mogul, concentrated his efforts in the Northeast of the country and was largely uninvolved in Florida. (C) Henry Flagler (1830-1913) was a Floridian involved in railways and oil production but is more closely associated with Miami than Orlando. (D) J.P. Morgan (1837-1913) was a New York-based banker.

54. **Which industry is not a part of the Florida economy?**
    (Skill 1.9) (Rigorous)

    A. Paper

    B. Electronics

    C. Steel

    D. Space and ocean exploration

Answer: C. Steel

The steel industry is located in various parts of the country, mostly in the East and Midwest. Such industries as paper and paper products, chemicals, electronics, and ocean and space exploration gave a tremendous boost to the labor force. From the 1950s to the present day, The Kennedy Space Center at Cape Canaveral has been a space and rocket center with the launching of orbiting satellites, manned space flights and today's space shuttles.

55. **An area of lowlands formed by soil and sediment at the mouths of**
    rivers is a (an):
    (Skill 2.1) (Rigorous)

    A. Needle

    B. Key

    C. Delta

    D. Mauna

Answer: C. Delta

A Delta is an area of lowlands formed by soil and sediment at the mouths of rivers

56. **Which is not on the North American continent:**
(Skill 2.1) (Easy)

    A. Mt. St. Helen's

    B. The Himalayas

    C. Mt. Everest

    D. Pike's Peak

Answer: B. The Himalayas

(B) The Himalayas are not on the North American and are located in Asia. (A) Mt. St. Helen's, an active volcano located in the state of Washington, is 8,364 feet in elevation since its eruption in 1980. (D) Pike's Peak, located in Colorado, is 14,100 feet in elevation. (C) Mt. Everest, in the Himalayan Mountains between China and Tibet is the highest point on the earth at 29,035 feet but is not located in North America.

57. **A physical geographer would be concerned with which of the following groups of terms?**
(Skill 2.2) (Rigorous)

    A. Low latitudes, precipitation, steppe

    B. Scarcity, goods, services

    C. Nation, state, administrative subdivision

    D. Cause and effect, innovation, exploration

Answer: A. Low latitudes, precipitation, and steppe.

(A) Low latitudes, precipitation, and steppe are all terms used in the study of geography. A landform is a physical feature of the earth, such as a hill or valley. A biome is a large community of plants or animals, such as a forest. Precipitation is the moisture that falls to earth as rain or snow. (B) Scarcity, goods, and services are terms encountered in economics. (C) Nation, state, and administrative subdivision are terms used in political science. (D) Cause and effect, innovation, and exploration are terms in developmental psychology.

58. **What is a tundra?**
(Skill 2.2) (Average)

   A. A narrow ridge of sand, gravel, and boulders deposited by a stream flowing on, in, or under a nonmoving glacier

   B. Accumulated earth, pebbles, and stones carried by and then deposited by a glacier

   C. The active front face of a non-stagnant glacier

   D. A marshy plain

Answer: D. A marshy plain

The word "tundra" meaning "marshy plain" is a Russian word and aptly describes the climatic conditions in the northern areas of Russia, Europe, and Canada. Winters are extremely cold and very long. Most of the year the ground is frozen but becomes rather mushy during the very short summer months. Surprisingly less snow falls in the area of the tundra than in the eastern part of the United States. However, due to the harshness of the extreme cold, very few people live there and no crops can be raised. Despite having a small human population, many plants and animals are found there.

59. **Where are there only two Seasons?**
(Skill 2.2) (Rigorous)

   A. The Prairies

   B. Savannas

   C. The Middle latitudes

   D. The Marine climate

Answer: B. Savannas

North and south of the tropical rainforests are the tropical grasslands called "savannas," the "lands of two seasons"--a winter dry season and a summer wet season.

60. **Which of the following is NOT a type of climate:**
    (Skill 2.2) (Average)

    A. Subtropical

    B. Marine

    C. Adiabatic

    D. Vertical climate

Answer: C. Adiabatic

(A) Subtropical, (B) marine and (D) vertical are all terms that relate to climate. (C) Adiabatic is a term used in physics and is not a type of rainfall.

61. **The Mediterranean type climate is characterized by:**
    (Skill 2.2) (Average)

    A. Hot, dry summers and mild, relatively wet winters

    B. Cool, relatively wet summers and cold winters

    C. Mild summers and winters, with moisture throughout the year

    D. Hot, wet summers and cool, dry winters

Answer: A. Hot, dry summers and mild, relatively wet winters

Westerly winds and nearby bodies of water create stable weather patterns along the west coasts of several continents and along the coast of the Mediterranean Sea, after which this type of climate is named. Temperatures rarely fall below the freezing point and have a mean between 70 and 80 degrees F in the summer. Stable conditions make for little rain during the summer months.

62.	The climate of Southern Florida is the _____ type.
(Skill 2.2) (Easy)

A.	Humid subtropical

B.	Marine West Coast

C.	Humid continental

D.	Tropical wet-dry

Answer: A. Humid subtropical

The (B) marine west coast climate is found on the western coasts of continents. Florida is on the eastern side of North America. The (C) humid continental climate is found over large land masses, such as Europe and the American Midwest, not along coasts such as where Florida is situated. The (D) tropical wet-dry climate occurs within about 15 degrees of the equator, in the tropics. Florida is sub-tropical. Florida is in a (A) humid subtropical climate, which extends along the East Coast of the United States to about Maryland, and along the gulf coast to northeastern Texas.

63.	Which is not a reason for different climate regions?
(Skill 2.2) (Easy)

A.	Latitude

B.	The amount of moisture

C.	The time of day

D.	Temperatures on land and water

Answer: C. The time of day

There are four reasons for the different climate regions on the earth are differences in: latitude, the amount of moisture, temperatures in land and water, and the earth's land surface.

64. **We can credit modern geography with which of the following?**
   (Skill 2.3) (Average)

   A. Building construction practices designed to withstand earthquakes

   B. Advances in computer cartography

   C. Better methods of linguistic analysis

   D. Making it easier to memorize countries and their capitals

Answer: B. Advances in computer cartography.

(B) Cartography is concerned with the study and creation of maps and geographical information and falls under the social science of geography.

65. **Which of the following is not a continent?**
   (Skill 2.3) (Easy)

   A. Asia

   B. Russia

   C. Europe

   D. North America

Answer: B. Russia

Russia is part of the continent of Europe.

66.   The continent of North America includes all but which of the
      following countries:
      (Skill 2.3) (Easy)

      A. Canada

      B. Mexico

      C. Cuba

      D. Ecuador

Answer: D. Ecuador

North America consists of (A) Canada; the United States of America; (B) Mexico;
the Caribbean island nations of the West Indies including (C) Cuba, Jamaica,
Haiti and the Dominican Republic; and the "land bridge" of Middle America,
including Panama, Honduras, El Salvador, Nicaragua, Guatemala, and others.
(D) Ecuador is a part of South America.

67.   If geography is the study of how human beings live in relationship to the earth on which they live, why do geographers include physical geography within the discipline?
(Skill 2.4) (Average)

A. The physical environment serves as the location for the activities of human beings

B. No other branch of the natural or social sciences studies the same topics

C. The physical environment is more important than the activities carried out by human beings

D. It is important to be able to subdue natural processes for the advancement of humankind

Answer: A. The physical environment serves as the location for the activities of human beings.

Cultures will develop different practices depending on the predominant geographical features of the area in which they live. Cultures that live along a river will have a different kind of relationship to the surrounding land than those who live in the mountains, for instance. Answer (A) best describes why physical geography is included in the social science of geography. Answer (B) is false, as physical geography is also studied under other natural sciences (such as geology.) Answers (C) and (D) are matters of opinion and do not pertain to the definition of geography as a social science.

68. **A cultural geographer is investigating the implications of <u>The Return of the Native</u> by Thomas Hardy. He or she is most likely concentrating on: (Skill 2.4) (Rigorous)**

   A. The reactions of British city-dwellers to the in-migration of French professionals

   B. The activities of persons in relation to poorly drained, coarse-soiled land with low-lying vegetation

   C. The capacity of riverine lands to sustain a population of edible amphibians

   D. The propagation of new crops introduced by settlers from North America

Answer: B. The activities of persons in relation to poorly drained, coarse-soiled land with low-lying vegetation

Thomas Hardy's novel <u>The Return of the Native</u> takes place in England, in a fictional region based on Hardy's home area, Dorset. Hardy describes the people and landscape of this area, which is primarily heath. A heath is a poorly drained, coarse-soiled land with low-lying vegetation, as described in answer (B). This is the most likely concentration for a cultural geographer studying Hardy's novel.

69. **Which of the following is not a concurrent power? (Skill 3.2) (Average)**

   A. Power to tax

   B. Power to declare war

   C. Power to borrow money

   D. Power to establish courts

Answer: B. Power to declare war

Concurrent powers are those powers that are granted to both the federal government and to the states. Both levels can (A) tax, (C) borrow money and (D) establish court. Only the federal government has the (B) power to declare war.

70. **Which of the following is not a branch of the federal government?**
(Skill 3.2) (Easy)

   A. Executive

   B. Legislative

   C. Judicial

   D. Vehicle Registration

Answer: D. Vehicle Registration

Vehicle registration is not a department of the federal government. It is a function and a part of the state governments.

71. **Which is not a power reserved to the states?**
(Skill 3.2) (Average)

   A. To coin money

   B. To regulate intrastate trade

   C. Enacting state and local laws

   D. Establish local governments

Answer: A. To coin money

The power to coin money is a power reserved to the federal government, not to the states.

72. **Which of the following is (are) powers delegated to the federal government?**
(Skill 3.2) (Average)

   A. To borrow and coin money

   B. To raise and support armed forces

   C. To fix standards of weights and standards

   D. All of these are powers delegated to the federal government

Answer: D. All of these are powers delegated to the federal government

The federal government has the authority to do all of theses things.

73. **Which branch is responsible for carrying out the laws of the country?**
(Skill 3.2) (Average)

   A. Judicial

   B. Executive

   C. Legislative

   D. Supreme Court

Answer: B. Executive

In the United States, the three branches of the federal government mentioned earlier, the **Executive**, the **Legislative**, and the **Judicial**, divide up their powers thus:

Article 2 of the Constitution created the (B) Executive branch of the government, headed by the President, who leads the country, recommends new laws, and can veto bills passed by the legislative branch. As the chief of state, the President is responsible for carrying out the laws of the country and the treaties and declarations of war passed by the legislative branch.

74. **Which branch established the power of the Supreme Court?**
     (Skill 3.2) (Easy)

     A. Judicial

     B. Executive

     C. Legislative

     D. House of Representatives

Answer: A. Judicial

In the United States, the three branches of the federal government mentioned earlier, the **Executive**, the **Legislative**, and the **Judicial**, divide up their powers thus:

Article 3 of the Constitution established the (A) judicial branch of government headed by the Supreme Court. The Supreme Court has the power to rule that a law passed by the legislature or an act of the Executive branch is illegal and unconstitutional.

75. **The _____ branch of government is made up of House of**
     Representatives and the Senate.
     (Skill 3.2) (Easy)

     A. Judicial

     B. Executive

     C. Legislative

     D. Supreme Court

Answer: C. Legislative

In the United States, the three branches of the federal government mentioned earlier, the **Executive**, the **Legislative**, and the **Judicial**, divide up their powers thus:

Article 1 of the Constitution established the (C) legislative, or law-making branch of the government called the Congress. It is made up of two houses, the House of Representatives and the Senate.

76. **The nation's first political parties formed behind:**
(Skill 3.2) (Rigorous)

    A. Washington and Hamilton

    B. Jefferson and Hamilton

    C. Madison and Hamilton

    D. Jefferson and Hamilton

Answer: B. Jefferson and Hamilton

The two parties that developed during the early 1790s were led by Jefferson as the Secretary of State and Alexander Hamilton as the Secretary of the Treasury. This was the basis for the establishment of political parties in America.

77. **Which one of the following is not a function or responsibility of the US political parties?**
(Skill 3.2) (Average)

    A. Conducting elections or the voting process

    B. Obtaining funds needed for election campaigns

    C. Choosing candidates to run for public office

    D. Making voters aware of issues and other public affairs information

Answer: A. Conducting elections or the voting process

The US political parties have numerous functions and responsibilities. Among them are obtaining funds needed for election campaigns, choosing the candidates to run for office, and making voters aware of the issues. The political parties, however, do not conduct elections or the voting process, as that would be an obvious conflict of interest.

78. **The U.S. Constitution, adopted in 1789, provided for:**
    (Skill 3.2) (Rigorous)

    A. Direct election of the President by all citizens

    B. Direct election of the President by citizens meeting a standard of wealth

    C. Indirect election of the President by electors

    D. Indirect election of the President by the U.S. Senate

Answer: C. Indirect election of the President by electors

The United States Constitution has always arranged for the indirect election of the President by electors. The question, by mentioning the original date of adoption, might mislead someone to choose B, but while standards of citizenship have been changed by amendment, the President has never been directly elected. Nor does the Senate have anything to do with presidential elections. The House of Representatives, not the Senate, settles cases where neither candidate wins in the Electoral College.

79. **In the Constitutional system of checks and balances, a primary "check" which accrues to the President is the power of:**
    (Skill 3.2) (Rigorous)

    A. Executive privilege

    B. Approval of judges nominated by the Senate

    C. Veto of Congressional legislation

    D. Approval of judged nominated by the House of Representatives

Answer: C. Veto of Congressional legislation
The power to (C) veto congressional legislation is granted to the U.S. President in Article I of the Constitution, which states that all legislation passed by both houses of the Congress must be given to the president for approval. This is a primary check on the power of the Congress by the President. The Congress may override a presidential veto by a two-thirds majority vote of both houses, however. (A) Executive privilege refers to the privilege of the president to keep certain documents private. Answers (B) and (D) are incorrect, as Congress does not nominate judges. This is a presidential power.

80. **The Bill of Rights was mostly written by:**
     (Skill 3.4) (Rigorous)

     A.   Thomas Jefferson

     B.   James Madison

     C.   George Washington

     D.   Alexander Hamilton

Answer: B. James Madison

The Bill of Rights, along with the majority of the Constitution, was mostly written by James Madison. Thomas Jefferson wrote the Declaration of Independence. Washington and Hamilton were present at the Constitutional Convention of 1787 in Philadelphia and they were advocates of federalism or increasing the power of the federal government.

81. **Gerrymandering applies to:**
     (Skill 3.4) (Rigorous)

     A. All elections

     B. National elections

     C. Local elections

     D. Adjusting electoral districts to achieve a goal

Answer: D. Adjusting electoral districts to achieve a goal

Gerrymandering refers to adjusting or designing electoral districts in a way that it brings about a predetermined outcome.

82. In the Presidential Election of 1888, Grover Cleveland lost to Benjamin Harrison, although Cleveland received more popular votes. How is this possible?
(Skill 3.4) (Rigorous)

A. The votes of certain states (New York, Indiana) were thrown out because of voting irregularities

B. Harrison received more electoral votes than Cleveland

C. None of the party candidates received a majority of votes, and the House of Representatives elected Harrison according to Constitutional procedures

D. Because of accusations of election law violations, Cleveland withdrew his name and Harrison became President

Answer: B. Harrison received more electoral votes than Cleveland

Presidential elections, according to the United States Constitution, are decided in the Electoral College. This college mirrors the composition of the House of Representatives. The popular vote for each presidential candidate determines which slate of electors in each state is selected. Thus, while Cleveland won enough support in certain states to win a majority of the national popular vote, he did not win enough states to carry the Electoral College. If neither candidate had won the necessary majority, the House of Representatives would have made the final decision, but this did not occur in 1888. The other two answers are not envisioned by the Constitution and did not occur.

83. **What was not one of the factors leading to the American Revolution? (Skill 3.6) (Average)**

    A. The desire to be an imperial Force

    B. Belief in equality

    C. Belief in no taxation without Representation

    D. The desire for freedom

Answer: A. The desire to be an imperial force

The colonists entered into the Revolution because of their beliefs in (B) equality and (C) no taxation without representation and the (D) desire for freedom. They did not have any (A) imperialistic desires.

84. **The term that best describes how the Supreme Court can block laws that may be unconstitutional from being enacted is: (Skill 3.7) (Rigorous)**

    A. Jurisprudence

    B. Judicial Review

    C. Exclusionary Rule

    D. Right of Petition

Answer: B. Judicial Review

(A) Jurisprudence is the study of the development and origin of law. (B) Judicial review is the term that best describes how the Supreme Court can block laws that they deem as unconstitutional as set forth in Marbury vs Madison. The (C) "exclusionary rule" is a reference to the Fourth Amendment of the Constitution and says that evidence gathered in an illegal manner or search must be thrown out and excluded from evidence. There is nothing called the (D) "Right of Petition", however the Petition of Right is a reference to a statement of civil liberties sent by the English Parliament to Charles I in 1628.

85. **Which legislation promoted settlement in the West?**
    (Skill 3.7) (Average)

    A. Quartering Act

    B. Missouri Compromise

    C. 1862 Homestead Act

    D. Compromise of 1850

Answer: C. 1862 Homestead Act

The Homestead Act opened the West to settlement by giving free land to settlers.

86. **What Supreme Court ruling dealt with the issue of civil rights?**
    (Skill 3.8) (Average)

    A. Jefferson vs Madison

    B. Lincoln vs Douglas

    C. Dred Scott v. Sanford

    D. Marbury vs Madison

Answer: C. Dred Scott v. Sanford

Marbury vs Madison established the principal of judicial review. The Supreme Court ruled that it held no authority in making the decision (regarding Marbury's commission as Justice of the Peace in District of Columbia) as the Supreme Court's jurisdiction (or lack thereof) in the case, was conflicted with Article III of the Constitution. (D) The Dred Scot case is the well-know civil rights case that had to do with the rights of the slave.

87. **Which concept is not embodied as a right in the First Amendment to the U.S. Constitution?**
    (Skill 3.11) (Rigorous)

    A. Peaceable assembly

    B. Protection against unreasonable search and seizure

    C. Freedom of speech

    D. Petition for redress of grievances

Answer: B. Protection against unreasonable search and seizure

The first amendment to the Constitution reads, "Congress shall make no law respecting an establishment of religion, or prohibiting the free exercise thereof; or abridging the (C) freedom of speech, or of the press; or the right of the people (A) peaceably to assemble, and to (D) petition the government for a redress of grievances." The protection against (B) unreasonable search and seizure is a constitutional right, however it is found in the fourth amendment, not the first.

88. **According to the Constitution any amendment must be ratified by _____ of the states to become a part of the Constitution:**
    (Skill 3.11) (Average)

    A. Three-fourths

    B. Two-thirds

    C. Three-fifths

    D. Five-sixths

Answer: A. Three-fourths

Article V of the Constitution spells out how the document may be ratified. First, an amendment must be proposed by a two-thirds majority of both houses of Congress. Then it is passed to the state legislatures. If (A) three-fourths of the states pass the amendment, it is adopted as part of the constitution. The constitution currently has 27 amendments.

89. **Collectively, the first ten Amendments to the Constitution are known as the:**
    (Skill 3.11) (Easy)

    A. Articles of Confederation

    B. Mayflower Compact

    C. Bill of Rights

    D. Declaration of the Rights of Man

Answer: C. Bill of Rights

The (A) Articles of Confederation was the document under which the thirteen colonies of the American Revolution came together and was the first governing document of the United States. The (B) Mayflower Compact was an agreement signed by several of the pilgrims aboard the Mayflower before establishing their colony at Plymouth in 1620. The (D) Declaration of the Rights of Man was the French document adopted after the French Revolution in 1789. The first ten amendments of the US Constitution, spelling out the limitations of the federal government, are referred to as (C) the Bill of Rights.

90. **In the United States, if a person is accused of a crime and cannot afford a lawyer:**
    (Skill 3.11) (Average)

    A. The person cannot be tried

    B. A court will appoint a lawyer, but the person must pay the lawyer back when able to do so

    C. The person must be tried without legal representation

    D. A court will appoint a lawyer for the person free of charge

Answer: D. A court will appoint a lawyer for the person free of charge

The sixth amendment to the Constitution grants the right to a speedy and public jury trial in a criminal prosecution, as well as the right to "the assistance of counsel for his defense." This has been interpreted as the right to receive legal assistance at no charge if a defendant cannot afford one. (D) A court will appoint a lawyer for the person free of charge, is the correct answer.

91. **An amendment is:**
     (Skill 3.11) (Easy)

     A. A change or addition to the United States Constitution

     B. The right of a state to secede from the Union

     C. To add a state to the Union

     D. The right of the Supreme Court to check actions of Congress and the President

Answer: A. A change or addition to the United States Constitution

An amendment is a change or addition to the United States Constitution. No amendment refers to states' abilities to succeed or be annexed or the right of the Supreme Court to check actions of Congress and the President.

92. **Which of the following is NOT considered to be a part of consumer economics:**
     (Skill 4.1) (Average)

     A. Consumers

     B. Economic systems

     C. Consumer behavior

     D. Price

Answer: B. Economic systems

The terms economic systems is a part of economics, but not of consumer economics. The term refers to how a society allocates its resources.

93. **Which best describes the economic system of the United States? (Skill 4.1) (Average)**

    A. Most decisions are the result of open markets, with little or no government modification or regulation

    B. Most decisions are made by the government, but there is some input by open market forces

    C. Most decisions are made by open market factors, with important regulatory functions and other market modifications the result of government activity

    D. There is joint decision making by government and private forces, with final decisions resting with the government

Answer: C. Most decisions are made by open market factors, with important regulatory functions and other market modifications the result of government activity.

The United States does not have a planned economy, as described in answers (B) and (D) where the government makes major market decisions. Neither is the U.S. market completely free of regulation, as described in answer (A). Products are regulated for safety, and many services are regulated by certification requirements, for example. The best description of the U.S. economic system is therefore (C) Most decisions are made by open market factors, with important regulatory functions and other market modifications the result of government activity.

94.   Capitalism and communism are alike in that they are both:
       (Skill 4.1 & 4.2) (Easy)

       A. Organic systems

       B. Political systems

       C. Centrally planned systems

       D. Economic systems

Answer: D. Economic systems

While economic and (B) political systems are often closely connected, capitalism and communism are primarily (D) economic systems. Capitalism is a system of economics that allows the open market to determine the relative value of goods and services. Communism is an economic system where the market is planned by a central state. While communism is a (C) centrally planned system, this is not true of capitalism. (A) Organic systems are studied in biology, a natural science.

95.   In a Socialist or Communist economy:
       (Skill 4.2) (Average)

       A. The open market determines how much of a good is produced and distributed

       B. The government owns the means of production

       C. Individuals produce and consume a specified good in whatever quantities they want

       D. The open market determines the demand for a good, and then the government produces and distributes the good

Answer: B. The government owns the means of production

In Socialist and Communist economies (B) the government owns the means of production and determines how much of a good is produced and distributed, as was the case in the Soviet Union and is still the case in Cuba and North Korea. A command economy is the opposite of a market economy, where (A) the open market determines how much of a good is produced and distributed.

96. **In a barter economy, which of the following would not be an economic factor?**
(Skill 4.2) (Easy)

   A. Time

   B. Goods

   C. Money

   D. Services

Answer: C. Money

A barter economy is one where (B) goods and (D) services are exchanged for one another and not for money. Just as in an economy with currency, (A) time is a factor in determining the value of goods and services. Since no money changes hands in a barter economy, the correct answer is (C) money.

97. _____ is the effort to create, by dictatorial means, a viable national society in which competing interests were to be adjusted to each other by being entirely subordinated to the service of the state although it will tolerate some private ownership of the means of production.
(Skill 4.2) (Rigorous)

A. Dictatorship

B. Parliamentary System

C. Anarchism

D. Fascism

Answer: D. Fascism

(A) Dictatorship is the rule by an individual or small group of individuals (Oligarchy) that centralizes all political control in itself and enforces its will with a terrorist police force. (B) Parliamentary System - A system of government with a legislature, usually involving a multiplicity of political parties and often coalition politics. There is division between the head of state and head of government. Head of government is usually known as a Prime Minister who is also usually the head of the largest party. The head of government and cabinet usually both sit and vote in the parliament. (C) Anarchism is a political movement believing in the elimination of all government and its replacement by a cooperative community of individuals. Sometimes it has involved political violence such as assassinations of important political or governmental figures. The historical banner of the movement is a black flag. But (D) fascism is a belief as well as a political system, opposed ideologically to Communism, though similar in basic structure, with a one party state, centralized political control and a repressive police system. It however tolerates private ownership of the means of production, though it maintains tight overall control. Central to its belief is the idolization of the Leader, a "Cult of the Personality," and most often an expansionist ideology. Examples have been German Nazism and Italian Fascism

98. **Which term does not apply to the stock market?**
    (Skill 4.3) (Average)

    A. Bull market

    B. Bear market

    C. Investors

    D. Black market

Answer: D. Black market

The stock market is an institution that (c investors take part in. (A) A bull market refers to a rising market and a (B) bear market refers to a falling market. (D) A black market is an illegal market.

99. **In a market economy, the price of a good is affected by:**
    (Skill 4.3) (Easy)

    A. Increase in demand and supply

    B. Decrease in demand and supply

    C. Degree of competition

    D. Prices are administered

Answer: D. Prices are administered

In a market economy, prices are determined by demand and supply and the degree of competition in a market. (D) Administered prices are fixed and are not consistent with a free market economy.

100. **Globalism refers to:**
(Skill 4.4) (Easy)

   A. Interdependence of all nations

   B. Independence of all nations

   C. Membership in the United Nations

   D. Autarky

Answer: A. Interdependence of all nations

Globalism refers to the fact that all nations are connected through the finance, trade and political events and what one nation does affect another. All nations are interdependent in today's world.

101. **Which organization is concerned specifically with international trade?**
(Skill 4.4) (Average)

   A. NATO

   B. United Nations

   C. SEATO

   D. WTO

Answer: D. WTO

The WTO is the World Trade Organization and it is concerned strictly with issue concerning trade between nations.

102. Civics does not encompass: (Skill 5.1) (Easy)

    A. Rights and responsibilities of Citizens

    B. Democracy

    C. Interrelationships between people

    D. Individual rights

Answer: C. Interrelationships between people

Civics is a study of government and the (A) rights and responsibilities of citizens. As such, it covers (B) democracy and (D) individual rights. It does not include a study of (C) the interrelationships between people.

103. Psychology is a social science because: (Skill 5.1) (Easy)

    A. It focuses on the biological development of individuals

    B. It focuses on the behavior of individual persons and small groups of persons.

    C. It bridges the gap between the natural and the social sciences

    D. It studies the behavioral habits of lower animals

Answer: B. It focuses on the behavior of individual persons and small groups of persons.

B. It focuses on the behavior of individual persons and small groups of persons. While it is true that (C) psychology draws from natural sciences, it is (B) the study of the behavior of individual persons and small groups that defines psychology as a social science. (A) The biological development of human beings and (D) the behavioral habits of lower animals are studied in the developmental and behavioral branches of psychology.

104. **A historian would be interested in:**
(Skill 5.1) (Average)

    A. The manner in which scientific knowledge is advanced

    B. The effects of the French Revolution on world colonial policy

    C. The viewpoint of persons who have written previous "history"

    D. All of the above

Answer: D. All of the above

Historians are interested in broad developments through history (A), as well as how individual events affected the time in which they happened (B). Knowing the viewpoint of earlier historians can also help explain the common thinking among historical cultures and groups (C), so all of these answers are correct (D).

105. **The sub-discipline of linguistics is usually studied under:**
(Skill 5.1) (Rigorous)

    A. Geography

    B. History

    C. Anthropology

    D. Economics

Answer: C. Anthropology

The fields of (A) Geography, (B) History and (D) Economics may study language as part of other subjects that affect these fields of study, but taken by itself language is a defining characteristic of a culture. (C) Anthropology studies human culture and the relationships between cultures, so linguistics is included under this social science.

106. **Which of the following is not generally considered a discipline within the social sciences?**
(Skill 5.1) (Easy)

   A. Geometry

   B. Anthropology

   C. Geography

   D. Sociology

Answer: A. Geometry

(B) Anthropology studies the culture of groups of people. (C) Geography examines the relationship between societies and the physical place on earth where they live. (D) Sociology studies the predominant attitudes, beliefs and behaviors of a society. All three of these fields are related to the social interactions of humans, and so are considered social sciences. (A) Geometry is a field of mathematics and does not relate to the social interactions of people, so it is not considered a social science.

107. **Economics is best described as:**
(Skill 5.1) (Average)

   A. The study of how money is used in different societies

   B. The study of how different political systems produces goods and services

   C. The study of how human beings use limited resources to supply their necessities and wants

   D. The study of how human beings have developed trading practices through the years

Answer: C. The study of how human beings use limited resources to supply their necessities and wants

(A) How money is used in different societies might be of interest to a sociologist or anthropologist. (B) The study of how different political systems produce goods and services is a topic of study that could be included under the field of political science. (D) The study of historical trading practices could fall under the study of history. Only (C) is the best general description of the social science of economics as a whole.

108. **Which of the following is most reasonably studied under the social sciences?**
(Skill 5.1) (Easy)

   A. Political science

   B. Geometry

   C. Physics

   D. Grammar

Answer: A. Political science

Social sciences deal with the social interactions of people. (B) Geometry is a branch of mathematics. (C) Physics is a natural science that studies the physical world. Although it may be studied as part of linguistics, (D) grammar is not recognized as a scientific field of study in itself. Only (A) political science is considered a general field of the social sciences.

109. **Which is not a main division of history?**
(Skill 5.1) (Rigorous)

   A. Time periods

   B. Nations

   C. Specialized topics

   D. Relationship to culture

Answer: D. Relationship to culture

History is the study of the past, especially the aspects of the human past, political and economic events as well as cultural and social conditions. This includes (A) time periods, (B) nations and (C) specialized topics. It does not include (D) relationship to culture.

110. **A political scientist might use all of the following except:**
(Skill 5.1) (Rigorous)

    A. An investigation of government documents

    B. A geological timeline

    C. Voting patterns

    D. Polling data

Answer: B. A geological timeline

Political science is primarily concerned with the political and governmental activities of societies. (A) Government documents can provide information about the organization and activities of a government. (C) Voting patterns reveal the political behavior of individuals and groups. (D) Polling data can provide insight into the predominant political views of a group of people. (B) A geological timeline describes the changes in the physical features of the earth over time and would not be useful to a political scientist.

111. **A geographer wishes to study the effects of a flood on subsequent settlement patterns. Which might he or she find most useful?**
(Skill 5.1) (Rigorous)

    A. A film clip of the floodwaters

    B. An aerial photograph of the river's source

    C. Census data taken after the flood

    D. A soil map of the A and B horizons beneath the flood area

Answer: C. Census data taken after the flood

(A) A film clip of the flood waters may be of most interest to a historian, (B) an aerial photograph of the river's source, and (D) soil maps tell little about the behavior of the individuals affected by the flood. (C) Census surveys record the population for certain areas on a regular basis, allowing a geographer to tell if more or fewer people are living in an area over time. These would be of most use to a geographer undertaking this study.

112. **A social scientist observes how individual persons react to the presence or absence of noise. This scientist is most likely a: (Skill 5.1) (Average)**

    A. Geographer

    B. Political Scientist

    C. Economist

    D. Psychologist

Answer: D. Psychologist

(D) Psychologists scientifically study the behavior and mental processes of individuals. Studying how individuals react to changes in their environment falls under this social science. (A) Geographers, (B) political scientists and (C) economists are more likely to study the reactions of groups rather than individual reactions.

113. **As a sociologist, you would be most likely to observe: (Skill 5.1) (Easy)**

    A. The effects of an earthquake on farmland

    B. The behavior of rats in sensory deprivation experiments

    C. The change over time in Babylonian obelisk styles

    D. The behavior of human beings in television focus groups

Answer: D. The behavior of human beings in television focus groups

Predominant beliefs and attitudes within human society are studied in the field of sociology. (A) The effects of an earthquake on farmland might be studied by a geographer. (B) The behavior of rats in an experiment falls under the field of behavioral psychology. (C) Changes in Babylonian obelisk styles might interest a historian. None of these answers fits easily within the definition of sociology. (D) A focus group, where people are asked to discuss their reactions to a certain product or topic, would be the most likely method for a sociologist of observing and discovering attitudes among a selected group.

114. **Which name is not associated with economics?**
(Skill 5.1) (Average)

   A. Adam Smith

   B. John Stuart Mill

   C. John Maynard Keynes

   D. Edward Gibbon

Answer: D. Edward Gibbon

(A) Adam Smith is considered to be the father of modern economics. (B) John Stuart Mill put forth the proposal of a more equal division of profits among employers and workers. (C) John Maynard Keynes wrote "The General Theory of Employment, Interest, and Money" in which he urged governments to increase their own spending in an effort to help end depressions, and he disagreed with the idea that free markets resulted in prosperity and full employment. (D) Edward Gibbon was a British scholar who wrote the masterpiece "History of the Decline and Fall of the Roman Empire". His name is not associated with economics.

115. **Cognitive, developmental, and behavioral are three types of:**
(Sill 5.1) (Average)

   A. Economist

   B. Political Scientist

   C. Psychologist

   D. Historian

Answer: C. Psychologists

(C) Psychologists study mental processes (cognitive psychology), the mental development of children (developmental psychology), and observe human and animal behavior in controlled circumstances (behavioral psychology.)

116. **An economist might engage in which of the following activities? (Skill 5.1) (Rigorous)**

    A. An observation of the historical effects of a nation's banking practices

    B. The application of a statistical test to a series of data

    C. Introduction of an experimental factor into a specified population to measure the effect of the factor

    D. An economist might engage in all of these

Answer: D. An economist might engage in all of these

Economists use statistical analysis of economic data, controlled experimentation as well as historical research in their field of social science.

117. **Political science is primarily concerned with _____. (Skill 5.1) (Easy)**

    A. Elections

    B. Economic Systems

    C. Boundaries

    D. Public Policy

Answer: D. Public policy

Political science studies the actions and policies of the government of a society. (D) Public policy is the official stance of a government on an issue and is a primary source for studying a society's dominant political beliefs. (A) Elections are also an interest of political scientists but are not a primary field of study. (B) Economic systems are of interest to an economist and (C) boundaries to a geographer.

118. **A social scientist studies the behavior of four persons in a carpool. This is an example of:**
(Skill 5.1) (Average)

    A. Developmental psychology

    B. Experimental psychology

    C. Social psychology

    D. Macroeconomics

Answer: C. Social psychology

(A) Developmental psychology studies the mental development of humans as they mature. (B) Experimental psychology uses formal experimentation with control groups to examine human behavior. (C) Social psychology is a branch of the field that investigates people's behavior as they interact within society and is the type of project described in the question. (D) Macroeconomics is a field within economics and would not apply to this project.

119. **A teacher and a group of students take a field trip to an Indian mound to examine artifacts. This activity most closely fits under which branch of the social sciences?**
(Skill 5.1) (Average)

    A. Anthropology

    B. Sociology

    C. Psychology

    D. Political Science

Answer: A. Anthropology

(A) Anthropology is the study of human culture and the way in which people of different cultures live. The artifacts created by people of a certain culture can provide information about the behaviors and beliefs of that culture, making anthropology the best-fitting field of study for this field trip. (B) Sociology, (C) psychology and (D) political science are more likely to study behaviors and institutions directly than through individual artifacts created by a specific culture.

120. **Which of the following is most closely identified as a sociologist? (Skill 5.1) (Rigorous)**

    A. Herodotus

    B. John Maynard Keynes

    C. Emile Durkheim

    D. Arnold Toynbee

Answer: C. Emile Durkheim

(C) Durkheim (1858-1917) was the founder of the first sociological journal in France and the first to apply scientific methods of research to the study of human society. (A) Herodotus (ca. 484-425 BC) was an early Greek historian. (B) John Maynard Keynes (1883-1946) was a British economist who developed the field of modern theoretical macroeconomics. (D) Arnold Toynbee (1882-1853) was also a British economist who took a historical approach to the field.

121. **Adam Smith is most closely identified with which of the following? (Skill 5.1) (Average)**

    A. The law of diminishing returns

    B. The law of supply and demand

    C. The principle of motor primacy

    D. The territorial imperative

Answer: B. The law of supply and demand

Adam Smith was an economist who developed the theory that value was linked to the supply of a good or service compared to the demand for it. Something in low supply but high demand will have a high value. Something in great supply but low demand is worth less. This has become known as (B) the law of supply and demand. (A) The law of diminishing returns is an economic principle described by Thomas Malthus in 1798. (C) The principle of motor primacy refers to a stage in developmental psychology. (D) The territorial imperative is a theory of the origin of property outlined by anthropologist Robert Ardrey in 1966.

122. **Margaret Mead may be credited with major advances in the study of: (Skill 5.1) (Average)**

    A. The marginal propensity to consume

    B. The thinking of the Anti-Federalists

    C. The anxiety levels of non-human primates

    D. Interpersonal relationships in non-technical societies

Answer: D. Interpersonal relationships in non-technical societies

Margaret Mead (1901-1978) was a pioneer in the field of anthropology, living among the people of Samoa, observing and writing about their culture in the book Coming of Age in Samoa in 1928. (A) The marginal propensity to consume is an economic subject. (B) The thinking of the Anti-Federalists is a topic in American history. (C) The anxiety levels of non-human primates are a subject studied in behavioral psychology.

123. **Of the following lists, which includes persons who have made major advances in the understanding of psychology? (Skill 5.1) (Rigorous)**

    A. Herodotus, Thucydides, Ptolemy

    B. Adam Smith, Milton Friedman, John Kenneth Galbraith

    C. Edward Hall, E.L. Thorndike, B.F. Skinner

    D. Thomas Jefferson, Karl Marx, Henry Kissinger

Answer: C. Edward Hall, E.L. Thorndike, B.F. Skinner

Edward Hall wrote in the 1960s about the effects of overcrowding on humans, especially in large cities. E.L. Thorndike (1874-1949) was an early developer of an experimental approach to studying learning in animals and of educational psychology. B.F. Skinner (1904-1990) was a pioneer in behavioral psychology. (A) Herodotus, Thucydides, and Ptolemy were early historians. (B) Smith, Friedman, and Galbraith made significant contributions to the field of economics. (D) Jefferson, Marx, and Kissinger are figures in political science.

124. The advancement of understanding in dealing with human beings has led to a number of interdisciplinary areas. Which of the following interdisciplinary studies would NOT be considered under the social sciences?
(Skill 5.1) (Average)

   A. Molecular biophysics

   B. Peace studies

   C. African-American studies

   D. Cartographic information systems

Answer: A. Molecular biophysics

(A) Molecular biophysics is an interdisciplinary field combining the fields of biology, chemistry, and physics. These are all natural sciences and not social sciences.

125. An anthropologist is studying a society's sororate and avunculate. In general, this scientist is studying the society's:
(Skill 5.1) (Rigorous)

   A. Level of technology

   B. Economy

   C. Kinship practices

   D. Methods of farming

Answer: C. Kinship practices

Sororate and avunculate are anthropological terms referring to interfamily relationships between sisters and between men and their sisters' sons. These are terms used to describe (C) kinship practices.

XAMonline, INC. 25 First St. Suite 106 Cambridge MA 02141

Toll Free number 800-509-4128

TO ORDER Fax 781-662-9268 OR www.XAMonline.com

FLORIDA TEACHER CERTIFICATION EXAMINATIONS - FTCE - 2009

PO#   Store/School:

Bill to Address 1   Ship to address

City, State Zip

Credit card number_____-_____-_____-_____   expiration_____

EMAIL _____

PHONE   **FAX**

13# ISBN 2008	TITLE	Qty	Retail	Total
978-1-58197-900-8	Art Sample Test K-12		$15.00	
978-1-60787-002-9	Biology 6-12		$59.95	
978-1-60787-003-6	Chemistry 6-12		$59.95	
978-1-60787-004-3	Earth/Space Science 6-12		$59.95	
978-1-60787-005-0	Educational Media Specialist PK-12		$59.95	
978-1-60787-006-7	Elementary Education K-6		$28.95	
978-1-58197-292-4	English 6-12		$59.95	
978-1-60787-007-4	Exceptional Student Ed. K-12		$73.50	
978-1-60787-001-2	FELE Florida Ed. Leadership		$59.95	
978-1-58197-619-9	French Sample Test 6-12		$15.00	
978-1-58197-615-1	General Knowledge		$28.95	
978-1-58197-586-4	Guidance and Counseling PK-12		$59.95	
978-1-58197-045-6	Humanities K-12		$34.95	
978-1-58197-640-3	Mathematics 6-12		$32.95	
978-1-58197-597-0	Middle Grades English 5-9		$59.95	
978-1-60787-008-1	Middle Grades General Science 5-9		$59.95	
978-1-60787-009-8	Middle Grades Integrated Curriculum		$59.95	
978-1-58197-284-9	Middle Grades Math 5-9		$59.95	
978-1-60787-010-4	Middle Grades Social Science 5-9		$59.95	
978-1-58197-616-8	Physical Education K-12		$59.95	
978-1-60787-011-1	Physics 6-12		$59.95	
978-1-60787-012-8	Prekindergarten/Primary PK-3		$73.50	
978-1-58197-695-3	Professional Educator		$34.95	
978-1-58197-659-5	Reading K-12		$59.95	
978-1-58197-270-2	Social Science 6-12		$59.95	
978-1-58197-583-3	Spanish K-12		$59.95	
978-1-60787-000-5	English to Speakers of Other Lang. K-12		$59.95	
			SUBTOTAL	
	1 book $8.70, 2 books $11.00, 3+ $15.00		SHIP	
			TOTAL	

CPSIA information can be obtained at www.ICGtesting.com
Printed in the USA
BVOW050502250613

324229BV00004B/285/P